THE ALLEN
ILLUSTRATED GUIDE TO
BITS AND
BITTING

THE ALLEN ILLUSTRATED GUIDE TO
BITS AND BITTING

HILARY VERNON

J. A. ALLEN · LONDON

British Library Cataloguing-in-Publication Data.
A catalogue record for this book is available from the British Library

ISBN 0.85131.725.1

Published in Great Britain in 1998 by
J. A. Allen & Company Limited,
1 Lower Grosvenor Place, Buckingham Palace Road,
London SW1W OEL

Design and Typesetting by Paul Saunders
Illustrations by Maggie Raynor
Colour Separation by Tenon & Polert Colour Scanning Ltd.(HK)
Printed in Hong Kong by Dah Hua Printing Press Co. Ltd.

This book is dedicated to my husband Andrew who has been subjected to years of relentless pressure to accept mud, wet rugs, hay in the kitchen and horses nearly always coming first. My heartfelt gratitude.

Contents

Acknowledgements

My mother Mrs June Vlies who has tirelessly supported me over the years and always encouraged me in every venture. Caroline Burt of J. A. Allen & Co. Ltd. who had faith in my idea. Richard Brown, Peter Phillips and all at Abbey Saddlery for all their invaluable help and for allowing me to use their catalogue pictures. Helen Archer for allowing herself to be used as a test reader and listening endlessly to ideas without being allowed to speak herself. Paul Brooker of Buxactic for cheerfully and promptly acknowledging my enquiries and giving all the help I needed to include Sprenger and KK bits in this book. Saddlery Trade Services in Walsall for all their help and literature on Happy Mouth bits. Alexe Etherington of James Cotterell & Sons Ltd for her time and information on The John Dewsbury range of bits despite the fact she has written her own bitting book. Sir David and Lady Checketts for allowing my equine family to reside at their home, and for their enthusiasm towards my venture. Doreen Govan who very kindly posted her bit measurer so that it could be copied and included in my book.

PART I

BITTING

Chapter 1

A Pre-bitting Logical Approach

Bitting is a complex and fascinating subject but, for all sorts of reasons, it can become very complicated. Not only is there a bewildering array of bits to choose from but nearly everyone you speak to has their own opinions and theories. Finding the right bridle and bit for your horse should be a blend of seeking obedience through correct schooling and the right degree of control, tempered with the rider's understanding of the horse's welfare and structural comfort. I feel that before deciding to change a bit we should first look at the wider picture. Resistances occur for all sorts of reasons, there are several points to be thought about before you decide that your horse has a bitting problem.

1. Is my horse completely comfortable in the mouth? Teeth checked recently?

You need to have your horse's mouth checked by a vet or an equine dental specialist at least once a year, starting at about three years old, or as soon as a bit is worn. A regular check for older horses is important because the horse's teeth continue to grow throughout his life and because of the direction that the horse's molars grow in. The molars do not meet evenly so are worn away leaving sharp edges on the outside edges of the upper jaw and the inside edges of the lower jaw. In the early stages this probably only means slight discomfort and some bruising but still results in an uncomfortable mouth for bitting

purposes. If the problem is not dealt with, the tongue and cheeks can be badly bruised and cut, taking time to heal and causing unnecessary mouthing and bitting problems. Signs that teeth may need immediate attention are as follows: general resistances to the bit which did not previously exist; obvious discomfort when a cavesson noseband is done up tightly, causing the horse's cheeks to be pressed onto the sharp edges of the teeth; reluctance to have the sides of the face handled; quidding, i.e. partially chewed food falling from the mouth and a general inability to eat up as normal; loss of condition. With a young horse you need to know that the mouth and teeth are formed properly so that the process of bitting will be a pleasant one or that, if there is a small problem, with a little thought, specialist treatment perhaps and the right bit, things can proceed as normal.

2. Does my saddle fit well? Is his back comfortable?

Saddles need fitting professionally in the first place and then flocking up and checking by a qualified saddler on a regular basis. Young horses change shape dramatically, as do new horses worked correctly for possibly the first time, older horses that have changed shape with the advancing years, or those who are coming back into work after a rest. This is a very specialist subject and with such a wide range of saddles on the market, a great deal of expertise is needed to get the horse comfortable and ready for work. An uncomfortable back can lead to many evasions that are nothing to do with the mouth and which no new bit is going to solve. Driving-harness saddle pads need to fit comfortably as well, particularly with two-wheeled vehicles, as a lot of weight is put on the horse's back when mounting and dismounting the vehicle. The well-stuffed padding should lie either side of the spine with the gullet of the tree itself clearing the spine, even when the full weight of the vehicle is pressing down.

3. Eating the correct food for temperament, work done, etc.?

If you are in a livery yard do you genuinely know what your horse is eating? Might a gradual change in feed bring about a more amenable animal? Some horses just do not need large amounts of protein and are too lively and unmanageable on several high energy feeds a day. We all know that to maintain good condition and to be able to do the work required, a horse must eat so many pounds per day for their body weight. But some horses are far better with small, low protein and high fibre feeds and good quality hay or good grazing. There are some excellent books on the subject that help you to gain a greater understanding of the subject. Most of the major feed firms have nutritionists only too happy to give helpful advice. All modern feed information is leaning towards less protein and more continuous ingestion of fibre as nature originally intended.

4. Getting out of the stable for an acceptable amount of time each day?

Enough freedom? Any freedom? Enough exercise? One hour's exercise with 23 hours in his box hardly seems fair when by nature a horse would wander about grazing freely for a good part of the day and night. A horse in a 12ft x 14ft (3.6m x 4.2m) stable

needs stimulation and occupation; haynets, exercise, and turnout must take up a great deal of his day so neither behavioural problems occur, nor the desire to misbehave at the slightest excuse when finally allowed out for some exercise. More exercise, haynets at regular intervals, a longer time in the paddock, plus perhaps even a fling free in the school for half an hour if no prolonged turnout is available, is better than nothing. Being turned out all night in the summer and all day in the winter could possibly change your horse's attitude to life in general.

5. Is the horse temperamentally suited to the work required?

There have been times when giving advice that I have thought that this is not the right animal for this job. You can feed, school and do everything to improve your horse's quality of life, and may well have very good results, but you cannot change personality. If a horse is calm and responsive by nature he is always going to be easier to handle and school than one who is very overreactive and highly strung. If you have your heart set on a particular equine sport then you must be realistic: you need to buy as near the perfect horse as possible. If you cannot bear to part with your friend, look again, change direction, do something you will both enjoy and maybe even excel at.

6. Is he old enough for the work expected?

There isn't a certain type of bit that will bring a young horse into a shape, or force it to maintain a head carriage. We should spend valuable time carefully bringing on young horses, so we can have years of pleasure. Two particular instances spring to mind. I was once asked what bit I would recommend to bring a three-year-old horse 'on the bit' and I was also asked to suggest a bit for a four-year-old horse whose rider had had to resort to a double bridle by the end of a four-day showjumping course as she could not stop! Bitting is not the answer if you have not established good basic groundwork with a young horse. A young horse's muscles are underdeveloped and he is unaccustomed to the weight of a rider. He needs time to learn to carry himself and the rider's weight and can be very heavy on the hand, leaning and trying to balance himself on it if allowed. He may take a long time to respond to the rider's aids. At this stage it is crucial that the rider allows him time to obey and learn, and does not assume that he is being disobedient, using harsher commands and bit changes to deal with it. It takes years of careful schooling to produce a really well schooled animal that can mentally and physically cope with the demands of competition. How many times do you hear people enthuse about a new youngster only to see him reach just half his potential. Choosing a bit to complement your young horse's make and shape is going to make it easier and more comfortable for him to learn what you are teaching. Every care should be taken not to damage a young horse's mouth. Once harmed, a youngster may become unwilling to accept the bit at all.

7. Is he fit enough for the work asked?

Resistance's due to a horse not being fit enough manifest themselves in different ways. Sharp horses can get very upset and begin to use speed and agitated behaviour as a way of saying they are uncomfortable. A stronger bit then makes the situation far worse, not better. If you are trying to pit strength against strength then the horse is by far the stronger. A more staid animal will perhaps be very heavy on the forehand, hanging on the hand, or bore down and snatch the rein. It is crucial that a horse is prepared for schooling and competition well. A horse that is tired and aching is not going to learn and carry out schooling exercises to the best of his ability.

8. Have I the right mouthpiece and cheek for the shape of my horse's mouth?

With all the different breeds, types and shapes of horses, not every one of them can be comfortable in the same bit. You need to study your horse carefully to make the right bitting decision. A lot of English-made bits can be made to order and a variety of mouthpieces can to be matched with different cheeks. It is possible, within reason, to get the mouthpiece that suits the shape of the inside of the mouth, with the cheek that gives the right degree of control, or suits your chosen discipline.

9. Does my horse have an easy conformation to bit?

Conformation of the head, jaw and neck has a great deal to do with the way the horse can accept a bit and do the work required. A short neck coupled with being thick through the jowl will make it difficult for a horse to flex properly. A ewe neck or a long underdeveloped neck is a weakness and will need careful schooling to enable a horse to comfortably maintain a good profile. A long or a weak back will need more ground work and strengthening exercises, resistance rooted here might lead someone to believe the problem is in the mouth when it is not.

10. Is he in any discomfort or pain caused by a badly fitting bit?

Any horse will resist if a bit does not fit properly, if his mouth is sore or if past experiences have prompted a habit to form. The horse's natural instinct is to run away from fear and pain. An open mouth, a tongue over the bit, a dry mouth or an overly frothy mouth are all signs of resistance or evasion of pain. The bars of the mouth are very sensitive and can easily be damaged, in really bad cases splints can actually form on the bars. The underside of the tongue can also be severely damaged if it is constantly over the bit.

11. Have I enough experience and ability to achieve my goals?

Bitting is not going to solve problems due to lack of rider or driver (whip) experience, or poor riding or driving ability. Becoming a competent and safe rider or whip takes time and practice, and at some time everybody needs to seek help from those correctly qualified to make a significant difference to their abilities. These days there is a wide choice of instructors and training centres to choose from and you need to select someone that suits your own personality and views. Getting to the top takes a lot of hard, dedicated work, a lot of hours in the saddle or on the box seat and a high degree of personal fitness. No severe bitting 'shortcut' is going to make a better rider and driver or a well-schooled horse.

12. Have I allowed enough time?

I have always maintained that it takes time to really get to know a horse. Unless you have bred him yourself you do not know what has happened in the past. For competing and even for just safely enjoying your riding, you need to establish a new horse's schooling, feeding and shoeing regime and find out all his little foibles. All this needs to be done in a calm and controlled environment. It is possible to rush things and cause problems by just being too keen to go to that first show or the opening meet or the driving club annual picnic. Even the most staid horse can become a real handful when faced with an exciting situation. If you have only ridden in a thick-mouth snaffle in a sand school and then suddenly find you are not in control, you may be tempted to change bits when more knowledge of your horse, more schooling and a better introduction to something new may be the answer.

Most of the subjects in this chapter could be covered in more depth and I have only touched on them lightly but, to summarise, a cooped up, over fed, uncomfortable young horse does not necessarily have a bitting problem at all, he may only need a change to create more comfort as opposed to more severity. So, when looking at bits and bitting the whole picture has to be taken into consideration.

Chapter 2

Pressure Points Explained Simply

Four pressure points within the mouth

The bars The bars of the mouth are the gum areas without teeth on the bottom jaw between the molars at the back and the incisors at the front of the mouth. They are very sensitive and the further forward you go towards the front teeth the narrower they are and the more sensitive they become. Breeding has a lot to do with the width and sensitivity of the bars. In a finely bred animal this area is very narrow and thinly covered with skin. In a thicker set or less finely bred animal the bars may be wider and have a fleshy covering making them much less sensitive. Steady pressure on the bars will normally make a horse lower his head. A careful check should be kept for cuts and bruising or teeth still in the gums. This area is easily damaged and great care must be taken because constant rough use can cause calluses and even splinter the bones. Any damage is ultimately going to make the mouth less sensitive.

The tongue This is a strong elastic muscle with a bump on it roughly halfway along situated approximately where the molars start. The tongue is often used by the horse to push against the action of the bit sending it forward in the mouth. The edges of the tongue are far more sensitive than the centre. Tongues come in all shapes and sizes, and need to be allowed to lie comfortably and naturally in the mouth without too much interference from the bit.

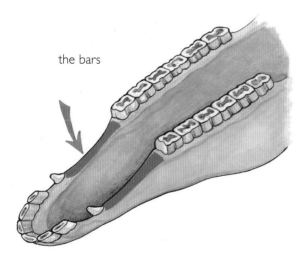

the bars

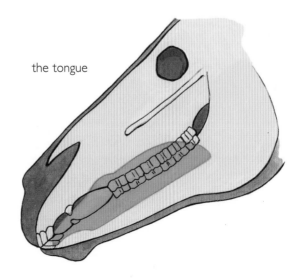

the tongue

Roof of the mouth Also known as the palate, this area is very soft and sensitive. Too much pressure here will cause the horse to try and alleviate it at any cost, either by opening his mouth or tipping the head over and tucking the chin into the chest. The structure of the roof can vary greatly and care needs to be taken that the bit chosen does not create unbearable pressure causing more problems.

Lips / corners of mouth Pressure on the lips and the corners of the mouth comes mainly from the snaffle, particularly the gag snaffle. This type of bit generally causes the horse to open his mouth and point the nose out. Continual pressure on the lip corners can cause soreness. Attention needs to be paid to the front molars of a horse wearing a gag because as the bit is drawn up into the mouth the corners of the lips and the inside of the cheeks are pushed onto the first molar teeth and can be cut if the teeth are too long or sharp.

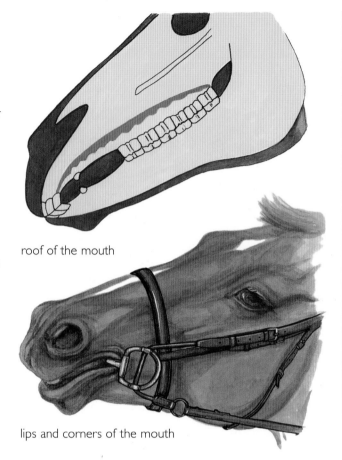

roof of the mouth

lips and corners of the mouth

Three external pressure points to the mouth

Chin groove There is a large, very sensitive nerve that runs down the edge of the underpart of the jaw and goes into the bone just above the chin. If the curb chain on a bit stays low in the curb groove as the bit is used, the horse should respond by flexing and relaxing the jaw but if the curb chain flips up out of the curb groove as the cheek of the bit is rotated, this moves pressure to the upper curb area and the action is then putting pressure on the sensitive jaw directly above the mandible nerve itself. This is a far more severe action and is very likely to cause resistance. The heavier the curb chain and the lower it stays when in use the better the result. It is quite possible to cause severe bruising to the curb area and in rare cases a splint can form with constant painful pressure.

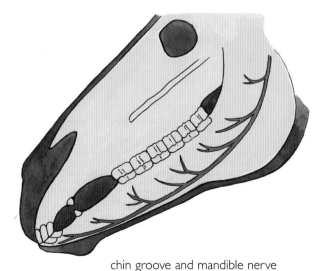

chin groove and mandible nerve

the poll area

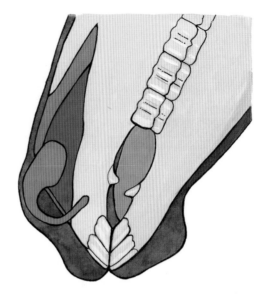

the nose area showing the cartilage

Poll pressure The poll area needs to be handled with care as all mechanical control relies on some form of bridle or head device fitting partially or fully to the poll region. Poll pressure by itself is not as significant as a lot of people seem to think, it is poll pressure combined with bit and/or nose pressure that gives the best results. If you push down on the top of a horse's head, his automatic reaction is to raise the head rather than lower it. It is also an area that is frequently and easily damaged often without an owner being aware of the injury.

Nose The nose is a very complex structure of bone and cartilage, it is very sensitive and easily damaged. It is easy to place nosepieces too low on the face making it uncomfortable and, more importantly, interfering with the horse's breathing. When anything is placed on the horse's head, care must be taken to fit it correctly; any noseband must be fitted high enough above the nasal cartilage to ensure comfort.

Chapter 3

Assessing the Structure of the Horse's Head and Mouth

The shape and length of the head, thickness of the lips, depth of the mouth, thickness of the tongue, height of the roof, position of the curb groove and width of the face, are all things that influence how each bit is going to work and fit, and how comfortable your horse is going to be. It is very important to check your horse's face and mouth on a regular basis so that you are alerted to any injury or abnormality instantly, and to know the mouth's inner structure.

Thick tongue The size of the tongue determines how each bit will work; the action of most bits is divided between the tongue and the bars of the mouth. With a thick tongue, the bit will touch the bars much later than it would with a thin tongue. To check just how thick the tongue is, part your horse's lips (with the teeth still closed), does the tongue appear to fill the mouth cavity and fill or even bulge out over the bars? If it does, there might not be that much room for a very thick bit or perhaps a combination of bits. In this situation you must think of creating more room: a single jointed snaffle might be changed for a French link snaffle, or a medium-ported snaffle. A show horse or cob might wear a Rugby pelham with a medium port instead of a double bridle thus allowing the tongue more room but still creating the illusion of a double bridle. The floating 'bradoon' ring can be attached to

a bradoon headpiece. With a dressage horse, possibly a French link bradoon with a medium-port Weymouth could be used. In short, with thought you can, within reason, follow the needs of your chosen sport and still ensure your horse is comfortable.

Low curb groove How low is the curb groove in relation to the corners of the lips? If there is quite a distance between the two it could mean that a curb chain or strap is going to flip up out of the groove and put all the pressure over the very sensitive mandible nerve that runs down the back of the jaw line. In this case perhaps a bit that does not have a curb chain, or a curb bit with a shorter top shank and a chain that is fixed lower on the cheek, would be the answer.

Short mouth How short is the mouth from the lip corner to the tip of the nose? The distance may be very short causing the centre joint of a jointed bit to hang too low and possibly in extreme cases even interfere with the front teeth. If your horse wears a pelham or Weymouth, a long shank is going to hang down well below the end of the mouth. A shorter cheek will make the overall picture look more in proportion.

Shallow bottom jaw A bottom jaw with plenty of depth can accommodate the tongue; as the horse feels pressure from the bit on the tongue it can move the tongue by flattening it into the floor of the jaw. But if your horse has a very shallow bottom jaw, a sensitive tongue has nowhere to go, unless it is drawn back or, in extreme cases, put over the bit. Again, a medium port or a French link mouthpiece could create a lot more room.

Narrow bottom jaw Some horses have very narrow bottom jaws; you can check this by making a fist and placing it between the rounded cheek-bones under the horse's face. If you have a very small hand (say a lady's size 7) and your hand fits, then the jaw is narrow. By checking a few horses you should be able to determine how narrow your own horse's jaw is. Care must be taken with the mouthpiece; the joints of a French link snaffle may end up in positions that interfere with the bars each side, or you may need to have a narrower bit than usual for a narrow-jawed horse.

Width of face With a triangular shaped face (narrow at the muzzle quickly getting wider) the use of pelhams and Weymouths can be made difficult. You need to find a bit with a short upper cheek (the part of the cheek above the mouthpiece) that is curved outwards to make sure it clears the face and does not rub or dig into the cheeks. A bit that has a 5in (12.5cm) mouthpiece may have to measure 6in (15cm) at the very top of the cheek piece eyelets to give a wide face more room. A sliding cheek has more movement than a rigidly fixed cheek and will angle out from the face a little better.

A very neat or tiny head This can look cluttered with a normal size snaffle ring, it is possible to put different sized bit rings and cheeks on a variety of mouthpieces so the horse can have the mouthpiece that suits the inside of his mouth with the cheek that complements the outside. A small pretty pony could have 2in (5cm) bit rings put on an ordinary snaffle mouthpiece to complement the face, without having to resort to a bradoon which usually comes on this size of ring and might prove to be too thin and severe.

Low roof A horse with a very low sensitive roof to the mouth will not be comfortable in a port that puts too much pressure on this area. A very low port should be used. Even a single jointed snaffle may touch the roof of some individuals too much and they may have to be bitted with very little or no pressure in this area. Possibly with a mullen or a low ported or a French link snaffle.

Corners of the lips These can very easily be made sore by over use and old injuries need careful consideration to avoid a recurrence. This is going to rule out most of the gags and any excessive lifting of the hands with a snaffle causing the bit to be pulled sharply into the mouth corners. In these cases a bit that acts more on the bars of the mouth and the tongue area will keep the action lower in the mouth and away from the corners.

Fleshy lips Very fleshy lips are difficult to accommodate and can easily be nipped or bruised by loose ring or sliding-cheek bits. With eggbut sides and fixed cheeks there is less risk of this happening. Bits must be wide enough and fit very well. A horse with very fleshy lips that is bitted with a curb-chained bit can get the extra flesh caught in the curb-chain hooks; a flat curb chain hook is a better alternative.

Chapter 4

The Use of External and Internal Aids

It must be remembered that the action of a bit can be enhanced by the use of a noseband or a training aid. But, and this is a big but, the action can also become drastically altered and very much more severe than you originally intended. So you must be careful, particularly if you are trying out a new bit, not to spoil the effect you are trying to create by altering the action.

Cavesson noseband If fitted for only cosmetic effect this noseband should lie two finger widths below the projecting cheek bone and you should be able to get two fingers between the band and the nose. Different widths can be used to good effect; a thin or a rolled nosepiece will complement a very fine delicate head, whereas a thick noseband on a long head can give the impression of a much shorter head. A thick band strategically placed can improve a nose with a bump in the wrong place. Fitted a little lower and fastened tighter, the cavesson can discourage the horse from opening the mouth too wide to evade the bit. In this case a thicker padded band should be used to distribute the pressure more evenly.

Crank noseband This noseband has several different names and slight variations of style but the principle is the same. The band is well padded and if fitted correctly the padding should almost meet at the back of the nose when the noseband is done up to the required tightness; the thinner non-padded

cavesson noseband

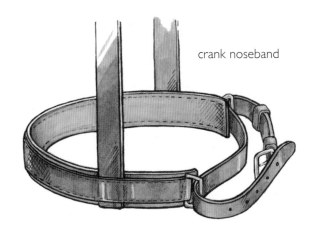

crank noseband

tightening strap does not touch the horse. When circumstances dictate that a flash or drop noseband cannot be used, with a double bridle for example, this noseband firmly fastened will help to dissuade the horse from opening the mouth to evade the bit. Extra padding can be put behind the noseband where the pressure is greatest to prevent rubbing.

Flash noseband The flash is really a cavesson with a detachable lower strap and should be fitted just like a cavesson but high enough so that the lower strap does not interfere with the horse's breathing. To have any effect, both bands must be fastened quite tightly. If you are relying on a tight noseband every time you ride you must make sure the horse is not getting rubs or calluses from the constant pressure. The lower strap should be done up on the side of the nose, which is much more comfortable for the horse, and not directly under the chin.

Drop noseband If fitted correctly, a drop noseband closes the mouth more effectively than any other aid. As the horse opens his mouth to evade the bit, a lot of nose pressure is created, this encourages the horse to drop his nose and relax the jaw to relieve the pressure. Care must be taken in the fitting of the drop; I have always had drop nosebands specially made. The ones usually available in tack shops are too long at the front of the nose and the back strap is always too short, making it impossible to fit correctly. The best 'shop bought' ones are the fully adjustable style that can be altered either side of the nose. It should be fitted with the front of the band above the nostrils on the solid part of the nose and not on the soft fleshy nasal cartilage, the back strap should angle down below the bit and fasten between the chin groove and the corner of the lip, to avoid any pinching.

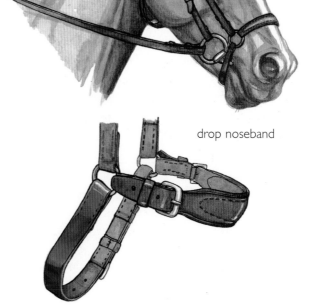

drop noseband

flash noseband

Grakle noseband This is an effective aid for upper and lower jaw pressure though not accepted by all disciplines. There are several different patterns of Grakle. The only one that works as originally intended is the one that adjusts on the nose (the straps can be moved through the nosepiece and are not riveted into place). By moving the straps through the nosepiece you are able to alter the pressure of the noseband up and down the face. The top strap should be fitted high, pulled up by the headpiece of the noseband, the bottom strap should slant down to fit below the bit.

grakle noseband

Kineton noseband The Kineton applies quite severe nose pressure; as the bit is pulled back in the mouth the noseband pulls back and down on the nose. Fitted like a drop noseband, the front piece should lie on the nose bone not on the nostrils. The metal loops fit under and around each side of the bit. The original Kineton pattern had a piece of metal set into the nosepiece for more severe pressure.

Kineton noseband

Bucephalus noseband

These two versions of the Bucephalus illustrate the same principle, both are normally secured to the middle of the bridle nose-band with a strap similar to a flash strap. The Bucephalus noseband then goes below the bit, crosses over under the chin and hooks onto the curb hooks of the bit. A version with hooks can also be hooked to the floating rings on a Wilson snaffle or into the top eye of a pelham or curb bit.

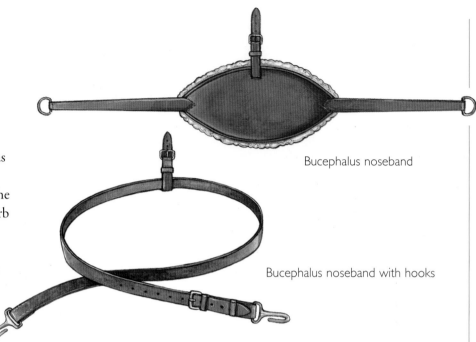

Bucephalus noseband

Bucephalus noseband with hooks

Bit guards Rubber bit guards are very useful for stopping the side of a bit from pinching the corners of the lips but they are not accepted in all disciplines. They come in a variety of colours from conventional brown and black to rainbow colours. To fit them you need to warm the rubber in hot water, tie baling string to the side of the bit and thread both bit guards over the string. Tie the string onto an overhead hook and pull each bit guard over the bit rings or cheeks in turn. This is by far the best way as forcing them over the side of a bit with long cheeks with a household spoon is almost impossible, and very hard on the fingers. For presentation driving harness, patent leather bit guards can complement the turnout; these are slit at the side for easy fitting.

Bristle bit guards These are designed to fit on only one side of the bit. The bristles encourage a reluctant horse to turn in a particular direction. If the horse is bad about turning right, the bristles are fitted on the left, and vice versa, thus making the horse move away from the discomfort. It is very easy to damage the skin on the face with the bristles.

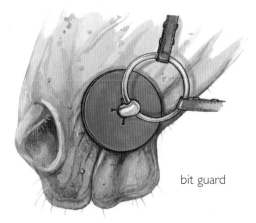

bit guard

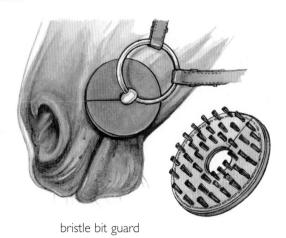

bristle bit guard

Tongue layer A tongue layer loops around the bit and lies on the tongue, pointing up the horse's mouth towards the back of the throat, to dissuade the horse from putting his tongue over the bit. Made of black rubber, they can be moved out of position by a determined horse and then possibly chewed.

Tongue grids Used on a bradoon headpiece and fitted above the bit, the grid lies on the tongue and, because of its shape, it is impossible for the tongue to be drawn back and over the bit. Made of wire and only in one size, a tongue grid is really a last resort for an habitual tongue problem.

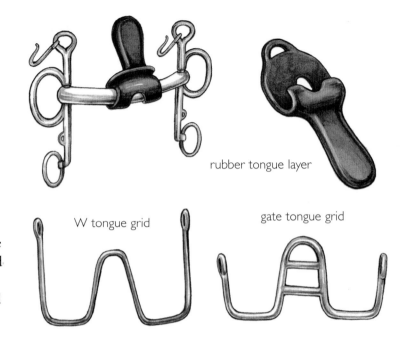

rubber tongue layer

W tongue grid

gate tongue grid

Chapter 5

Bit Accessories

As well as considering the structure and bitting needs of the individual and general comfort of the mouth, bit attachments and accessories need thinking about as well if all the horse's bitting needs are to be met. It is no good getting the inside of the mouth right if the corners of the lips are being pinched by a badly fitting curb hook. Or the curb chain that has been supplied with the bit is too severe for a particular horse.

Single-link curb chain This curb chain is not often seen these days because it is not as comfortable for the horse as the thicker double linked variety.

Double-link curb chain This is the chain that is issued with nearly all curb-chain-carrying bits today. They come in four standard sizes: small pony, pony size, cob size and full size though, if necessary, chains can be made longer than the standard full size. When fitting the chain you must twist it so that it is perfectly flat and make sure that when you hook it up onto the bit the links remain flat on the curb groove. Spare links can look untidy dangling from the side of a bit so the excess links can be nipped off with pliers providing that enough are left for adjustments to be made.

single-link curb chain

double-link curb chain

Flat link, or polo, curb chain The flat links cover more surface area than the ordinary double-link variety and is therefore more comfortable because it spreads the pressure load. The only possible drawback is that, on a horse with a very narrow curb groove, the chain may cause too much pressure on the more sensitive upper curb area.

Leather curb strap This is a very much kinder alternative to chain. The leather distributes the pressure evenly in a continuous strip, but requires more maintenance as the leather needs to be kept soft and supple all the time. They usually come in a fairly thick leather form but saddlers can make them up in soft bag hide on request.

flat link, or polo, curb chain

leather curb strap

Elastic curb strap Elastic is an even softer alternative than leather. As the curb strap comes into play, the stretch in the elastic means that there is more time before the full action of the curb is felt by the horse; an added bonus for a very sensitive horse. The strap must be kept very clean because the horse's saliva can make it go hard causing the curb groove area to be rubbed.

Jodhpur curb chain This is a severe curb chain. The large, shaped central link moves the pressure from the less sensitive curb groove, right onto the very sensitive jaw area where the mandible nerve runs down the jaw line with only a very thin layer of skin for protection. Severe pressure is brought to bear over a large area and must cause the horse pain if used carelessly.

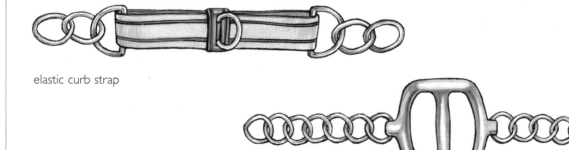

elastic curb strap

jodhpur curb chain

rubber curb guard

jelly curb guard

Rubber curb guard This is a very effective and inexpensive way of helping to soften the effect of a curb chain; the chain must be twisted flat then the rubber curb protector slides over the flattened chain. Once encased, the chain has to lie flat. It comes in several colours but black and brown blend in well with the leather of bridlework.

Jelly curb guard A very soft leather pouch filled with jelly buffers the effect of the curb chain, lying comfortably against the horse's skin. As with all leather goods it takes regular maintenance to keep it supple. Made in a soft, supple fine leather it moulds to the shape of the horse's face.

Flat, or circle, curb chain hooks The metal of the curb chain hooks usually supplied with a bit is inferior to the bit metal and they are frequently not very well made. The flat curb chain hook is of much better quality, lies more comfortably on the side of the face and there is a lot less risk of the corner of the lip being pinched. You can buy these separately and fit them to any bit yourself.

Bit snaps These are designed to enable you able to convert a leather headcollar into a bridle by attaching a bit to it. They have either a brass or steel finish to blend in with the stainless steel or brass cheek of a bit, or the headcollar fittings.

Bit straps These are used for the same purpose as above but are small leather straps, also with stainless steel or brass buckles to complement bit cheek or tack.

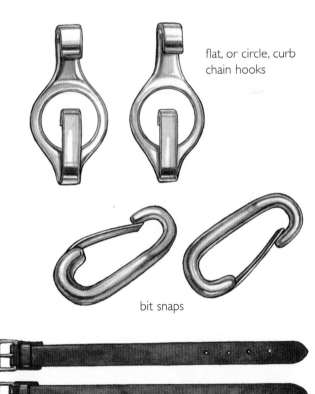

flat, or circle, curb chain hooks

bit snaps

bit straps

Lip straps These attach to small eyelets on the cheeks of either a pelham or Weymouth bit and run through the fly link in the middle of the curb chain at the back. They help to keep a curb chain in place and also preven the cheeks of a Banbury pelham or Banbury Weymouth from rotating too far. They come in either a flat or rolled pattern and are available in colours to complement your bridlework.

rolled lip strap

Pelham roundings If you are unable to use a pelham bit with two reins, roundings allow the use of only one rein by connecting the top 'bradoon' ring and the bottom 'curb' ring so that one rein can be attached to the rounding. This means there is an even pull on the bit with very little curb action.

pelham roundings

Fulmer keepers or guides These are small leather loops fitted from the cheekpiece of the bridle to the cheek of the bit, designed to hold the bit cheek in place and also stops the cheek going into the horse's nostril. The keepers Create a minimal amount of poll action. They are usually used only on Fulmer snaffles but can also be used on other cheeked snaffles.

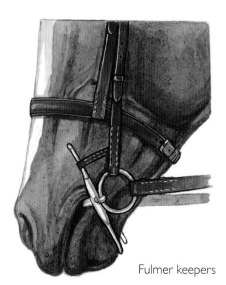

Fulmer keepers

Australian Cheeker This pulls the bit up towards the roof of the mouth to help prevent the tongue from being put over the bit. It attaches to the top of the bridle headpiece with a small strap.

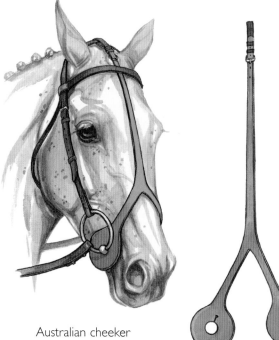

Australian cheeker

As the bit is used, the rubber nosepiece pulls back on the nose helping to reinforce the nose pressure,

Latex This is a thin self-sealing latex bandage. It was originally designed for American racehorses racing on wet racetracks because it does not absorb any moisture. Used as a wrap for bits it can just give a soft rubbery layer to a bit without making the bit very thick. It is very useful if you feel a horse would benefit from a rubber-covered bit, but know that he probably does not have enough room in its mouth for a thick bit. Care should be taken as latex is not completely smooth and can, in some horses, cause soreness. It can also be used to wrap in a figure of eight pattern on the cheek of a slide cheek bit to stop the play in the cheek or prevent pinching. It

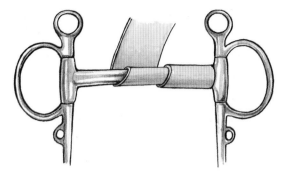

latex wrapping a bit

must be wrapped evenly and tightly so that the bit is the same thickness all the way along and that the layers are firm and do not twist or move. You can cut strips off to fit difficult places as long as the overall thickness is the same.

Chapter 6

Bitting Materials

Stainless steel There is a lot of foreign stainless steel on the market used for seemingly smooth lightweight bits. The manufacture of these bits is not, however, governed by strict manufacturing controls so the strength of these relatively inexpensive bits is very questionable. British steel is purer and far better made and therefore much safer. There is also a much larger range of bit and cheek sizes in British steel. You always get what you pay for and a good quality bit in your horse's mouth is a very important safety factor.

Rubber The core of the mouthpiece of a flexible rubber mullen bit is a substantial chain which for safety reasons is well attached to the cheekpieces. It is then covered with the rubber moulded mouthpiece. In a jointed rubber bit the core is actually a metal jointed bit with a less polished finish so that the rubber mould will stick to it successfully.

Vulcanite Covered mullen and jointed bits are ordinary metal bits left with a duller finish, so that the vulcanite mould will stick permanently to the metal.

German silver This is an alloy containing approximately 60% copper, and 12–16 % nickel and zinc. The copper content encourages horses to mouth the bit, thus stimulating the flow of saliva. German silver oxidates which produces a taste that seems to encourage this process.

Aurigan Containing 85% copper plus 4% silicon and zinc, aurigan is guaranteed nickel free. Some horses have been known to have an allergy to nickel which often appears as pimples in the mouth. The skin can turn red and become sore. Despite its high copper content it is a very robust metal.

Kangaroo This is an exclusive material using certain trace elements which are a trade secret but is predominantly made from 70% copper and 30% nickel. Bits made from this metal are very strong and durable with excellent mouthing qualities owing to the copper content; this encourages the horse to accept the bit and move forward. Some bit ranges are very limited but there is an extensive well-made range available in kangaroo metal.

Copper Although a very soft metal, copper has very good mouthing qualities but is only used in the construction of mouthpieces or parts of mouthpieces as it wears very easily and needs constant monitoring to make sure the bit remains safe. The cheeks of copper bits are usually made from stainless steel for strength.

Happy Mouth Bit mouthpieces made from this material have stainless steel rings and cheeks, with either a solid stainless steel or twisted steel wire core. The mouthpiece is made from a non-toxic, apple-scented, flexible engineered plastic. This is not as pliable as some of the non-metal materials but provides a much larger range than most.

Aluminium bronze This very strong alloy produces a brass-look finish but is far stronger than brass and therefore much safer to use in the manufacture of bits. It is becoming more popular, particularly in the manufacture of driving bits.

Nathe Nathe is a very soft, pliable, off-white synthetic material which has a flexible inner core for safety. The fact that this soft material can be used without the bulk normally associated with rubber-type bits is a feat of engineering. It has a limited range of bit types and, as with all non-metal materials, a limited lifetime. To ensure as long a life as possible for these bits, the horse's teeth must be in very good condition.

Measuring

Mouthpieces are measured in ¼in (6mm) increments. Some of the snaffles start at 3in (7.5cm) but most of the bits range from 4in (10cm) up to 6in (15cm), but certain bits can be made with 8in (20cm) mouthpieces.

Pelham and Weymouth cheeks come in different lengths usually from 4in (10cm) increasing in ¼in (6mm) increments up to 7in (17.5cm), although longer cheeks can be made. Milder pelhams or Weymouth's can be created with shorter or Tom Thumb cheeks. The longer the cheek the more severe the action.

A lot of bit cheeks are interchangeable with different mouthpieces giving a wide variety of bit types and degrees of control.

It can be quite difficult to measure the horse's mouth. The usual method is to try different bits then measure the one that fits. Your local saddler may have a bit measurer; this is a measured bar marked in ¼in (6mm) increments all the way along. The bar is fixed one side and movable on the other and is suspended on a bradoon headpiece. The bar and headpiece is put on the horse like a bridle after the screw has been loosened on the movable side. When the bar is in the horse's mouth, the movable plate can be moved in until both smooth plates fit comfortably either side of the horse's face. One finger should fit sideways between the side of the horse's face and the cheek of the measure. Then tighten the screw, take the headpiece and bar off and read the measurement on the inside.

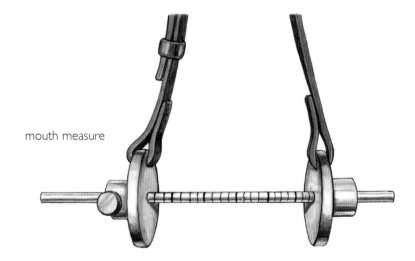

mouth measure

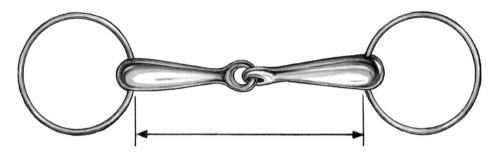

how to measure a loose-ring jointed snaffle mouthpiece

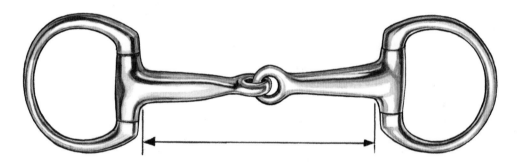

how to measure an eggbutt snaffle mouthpiece

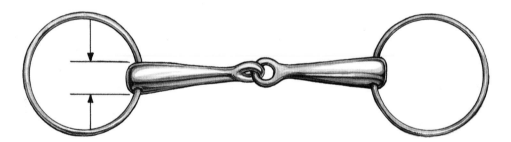

how to measure the thickness of a mouthpiece

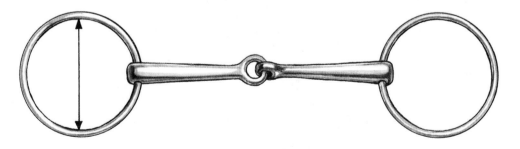

how to measure a snaffle bit ring

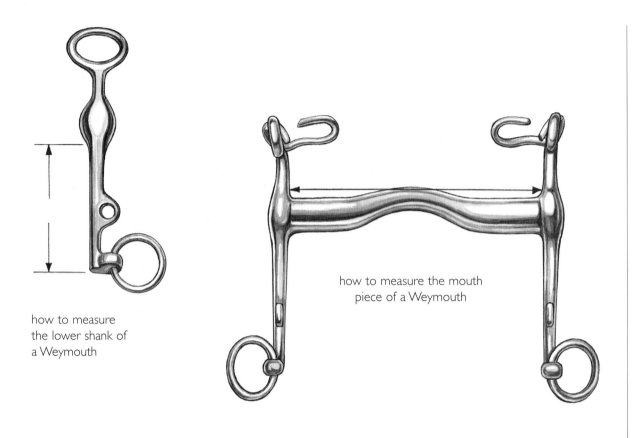

how to measure
the lower shank of
a Weymouth

how to measure the mouth
piece of a Weymouth

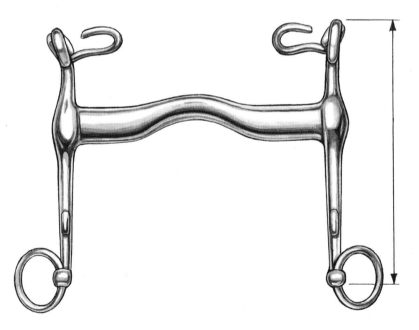

how to measure the full
shank of a Weymouth

How to Buy a Bit and What to Look for

OVER THE PHONE

Give the correct name for the bit that you want.

Asking for a 5in (12.5cm) Rugby pelham with a medium port and a 5in (12.5cm) cheek will instantly give the saddler an accurate and clear description of exactly which bit you want. Rather than 'Can I have a snaffle or a pelham?' to which the reply has to be 'Yes certainly but what sort of mouthpiece and cheek would you like?' In my experience the subsequent reply can often be 'Oh I don't know, what do they come with?'

If you are seeking advice, be able to state why you feel you need another bit and be able to describe how your horse is going.

In an ideal situation the adviser should be able to see you ride the horse and even ride him themselves but this is usually not possible. So your saddler can only give you advice over the phone if you can give a good description of what bit your horse is currently wearing, which, if any, bits have been tried in the past, how the horse is going and what sort of resistance is occurring.

Have ready a bit that fits the horse you are buying for and a tape measure.

Bit sizes can often vary as can people's conceptions of how to measure one. If you have the bit and a tape measure at the ready you can say 'I am measuring across the bit just inside the cheekpieces where the horse's mouth would be' or 'I am measuring from the very top to the bottom of the cheek and it is exactly 5 inches'.

GOING TO THE SADDLER

Take with you a bit that fits the horse you are buying for.

The saddler can measure the bit for size. With a new horse you could, perhaps, borrow the bit that he goes well in from the previous owner or from someone else who has a bit that fits him.

Give an accurate description of how your horse is going.

You still need to discuss the merits of different bits in relation to how your horse behaves. If this is a new horse, get all the information you can from the previous owner as to which bit the horse has worn and if they changed bits for, say, cross country or fast work.

WHAT TO LOOK FOR IN A BIT

- A smooth finish that feels comfortable to the touch.

- Cheekpieces that move freely.

- Central joints that are smooth and well joined in the middle.

- French links that are flat and not too long, with joints that are not too bulky.

- Ports that are wide enough to accommodate the horse's tongue.

- Rollers that roll freely but do not have any gaps that could pinch.

- A nice substantial feel; very lightweight bits cannot provide the subtleties of feel for the horse. When the rein is given with a heavier bit it is instantly felt by the horse and is a reward for correct work.

Chapter 9

How Different Bits Work

Riding and carriage driving can be very dangerous for many reasons so it is important to have good quality, well-made bits, tack and harness. But time and time again cheap and badly designed equipment is sold because the price is right or the buyer is not sufficiently informed to know the difference. So often these days equestrian equipment is designed and sold by people who have no sound equine knowledge. Sometimes it is possible, with care, to buy inexpensive things but I feel that when it comes to bits the only thing to do is to buy the best. If a bit breaks in your horse's mouth over a fence or during fast work or in heavy traffic just think of the consequences.

Bits are for controlling the speed of the horse, containing the impulsion created by the rider's seat and leg, for turning and stopping. Some bits are good at one job and not as good at others. People often expect too much of bits, forgetting that there are a lot of other things to be taken into consideration.

If you are thinking about trying out a new bit, remember that a horse needs time and schooling to get used to a new feel and respond to the basic action. It should always be used in a safe controlled environment such as a school.

Generally speaking, the thinner the mouthpiece the more severe it is and the thicker the mouthpiece the milder it is as there is more surface area to work on. If your horse simply does not have the mouth capacity to take a thick bit, however, then it is not kind to put one in his mouth. A very thick bit can actually stop a horse with a fine delicate mouth from being able to close it properly. A thinner bit of the right shape for your horse's mouth used correctly will achieve a far better result. Never forget that it is the hands on the end of the reins that do the damage.

Actions of different combinations of mouthpieces and cheeks

These days it is possible to match a large number of mouthpieces to different cheeks. What we have to remember is that this can dramatically alter the action of certain bits; teamed with one sort of cheek, a mouthpiece can be quite mild but with a different cheek the same mouthpiece can be extremely severe.

The following descriptions clarify bit actions.

Snaffle cheek All bits of the snaffle family work primarily on the corners of the lips even though some of them such as the hanging-cheek, the swivel and the beval snaffles all employ a little poll pressure but not to any great degree.

Leverage cheek This employs a leverage action only without a curb chain. The degree of leverage is determined by which rein position you use, the bottom one can be very severe.

Curb cheek This cheek also applies leverage but in conjunction with a curb strap or chain.

Gag snaffle The action of this bit depends on which rein you use. The bit rein, i.e. the rein attached to the bit itself, will give the action of a snaffle. The gag rein is attached to the gag cheek that runs through the centre of the bit ring and employs poll and corner of lip pressure.

SNAFFLES

Snaffle and bradoon bit rings come in a range of different ring sizes, 1½in (3.75cm) to 4in (10cm) rising in ⅛in (3mm) increments measured on the inside of the ring. The mouthpiece that suits your horse can, therefore, have the cheek that is in proportion to head size or, in the case of a youngster or a schooling problem, a cheek that supports your signals. The snaffle gives the horse the clearest signal to turn.

Hanging-cheek, beval and swivel snaffles all employ a certain amount of poll pressure. With the beval snaffle, the eyelets to which the reins and the cheeks of the bridle are fixed are small so the horse feels the action immediately. This has more poll action than the hanging-cheek snaffle.

Single-jointed mouthpiece with a snaffle cheek As the reins are pulled by the rider, the joint lifts up towards the roof of the horse's mouth creating a triangle, forcing the tongue into a V shape, pinching not only the tongue but the bars of the mouth as well. If the rider lifts the hand this puts more pressure on the corners of the lips and a lowered hand puts more pressure onto the bars, tongue and roof. An eggbutt cheek has a quicker and more defined action but a loose-ring cheek has more play (as the rein is picked up the mouthpiece slides on the cheek before the bit's action is felt by the horse). This is possibly a plus point if your horse is sharp as it gives him a second or two longer to absorb the signal you are giving him but it may also encourage playing with the bit as there can be a lot of movement between mouthpiece and cheek.

Mullen mouthpiece with a snaffle cheek This mouthpiece actively encourages a horse to

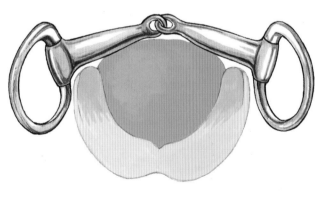

jointed snaffle in the mouth

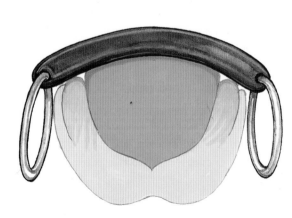

mullen in the mouth

move forwards and push his tongue against the bit if he has ample mouth room. This is very useful for a horse that needs confidence to go forward and take up more contact. The softer the material, the more encouragement is given. The drawback to a straight bar or mullen mouthpiece is that you lose the ability to use only one side of the bit, a particular problem when turning because as soon as you use one rein, the other side of the bit will move to some degree as well.

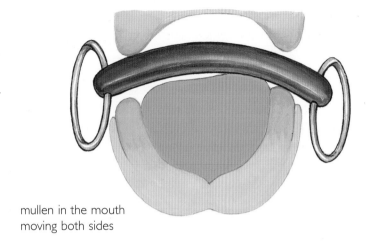

mullen in the mouth
moving both sides

Medium port with a snaffle cheek If your horse is not comfortable with a jointed mouthpiece or you are trying to create more tongue room or use the bars of the mouth more than the tongue, a medium port on a loose-ring snaffle cheek may be the answer. As the bit comes into play the tongue has plenty of room to move up and fill the space created by the port. The height of a medium port is not high enough to interfere with the roof of the mouth.

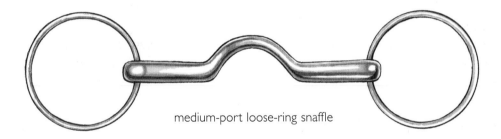

medium-port loose-ring snaffle

French link mouthpiece with a snaffle cheek The smooth, central shaped plate of this bit follows the line of the horse's tongue. It is important that the plate is not too long. It should be about 1in (2.5cm) in length and the joints should be as small and as smooth as possible. When the rein is used, the mouthpiece wraps around the tongue allowing far more tongue room than an ordinary jointed snaffle, taking a lot of pressure off the bars of the mouth and not pointing into the roof of the mouth.

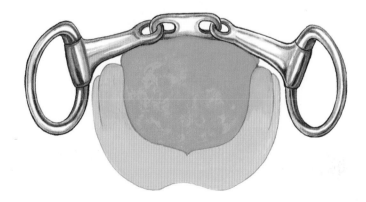

eggbutt French link in the mouth

Dr. Bristol mouthpiece with a snaffle cheek The central plate on this type of bit is set at an angle to the rest of the mouthpiece and is designed to press into the horse's tongue. Consequently, a horse who uses his tongue as a means of pushing against the bit and therefore taking control, will draw back and tuck his chin in, coming back to a better point of control. There are several incorrect designs of Dr. Bristol mouthpiece; the one that works as originally intended should have a flat not too thin oblong plate approximately 1in (2.5cm) long which is set at an angle to the rest of the mouthpiece and does not follow the line of the mouthpiece as a French link should.

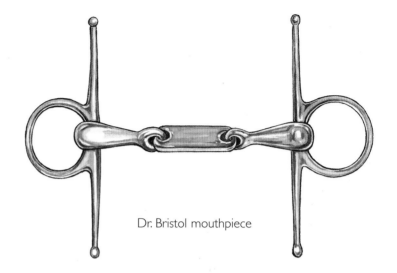

Dr. Bristol mouthpiece

Cheeked and D ring snaffles
The action of these bits will be the same as a single- or double-jointed snaffle but, as the bit is used to turn the horse, the cheek puts pressure on the side of the face encouraging the horse to turn. It also helps to keep the head straight. The Fulmer snaffle should always be used with a small leather keeper that loops over the upper cheek of the bit and attaches to the bridle cheekpiece. Used with a keeper, the bit creates a little poll pressure and keeps the cheek of the bit in place.

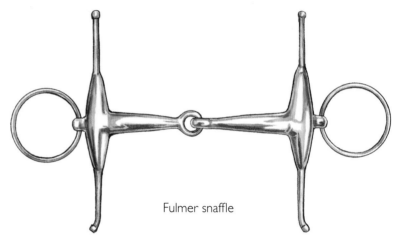

Fulmer snaffle

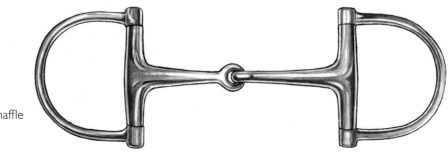

D ring snaffle

Roller mouthpieces Examples are cherry rollers and D ring copper rollers. As long as the bit is well made and the rollers are tightly constructed, the rollers roll in the horse's mouth giving him something to play with and reducing the likelihood of the bit being held in the horse's teeth. But however well made, anything that constantly rolls or rubs against something else is subject to extra wear. If you are going to use roller mouthpieces a constant check must be made on the tightness of the rollers as the slightest gap can cause severe injury to a horse's mouth. The bit action will be the same as described before depending on whether the mouthpiece is on snaffle or leverage cheeks. Both types of rollers can be made with straight bar and jointed mouthpieces.

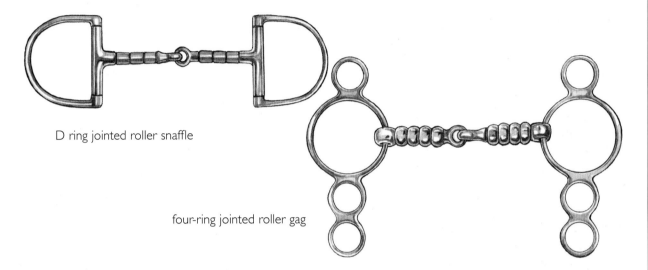

D ring jointed roller snaffle

four-ring jointed roller gag

DOUBLE BRIDLES

The double bridle, when used correctly, should only perfect and refine what the horse can already perform in a snaffle. Horse and rider need to be able to maintain correct balance before the introduction of a double bridle otherwise any weak spots in training will be accentuated not improved and subsequently be even more difficult to correct. Both bits have very different actions and generally speaking it is usual to put a slide-cheek Weymouth with a loose-ring bradoon and a fixed-cheek Weymouth with an eggbutt bradoon although this is a matter of personal taste and comfort for the individual horse. The bits are used and fitted as follows.

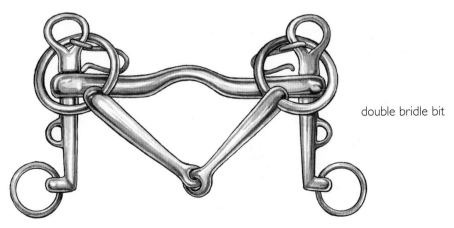

double bridle bit

The bradoon This is just a small snaffle fitted in the mouth above the curb or Weymouth bit and should in most cases be ¼in (6mm) longer than the Weymouth. The bradoon, like the snaffle, gives the horse the clearest signal to turn. It is usually quite thin and therefore has the potential to be severe.

The Weymouth This curb is fitted comfortably below the bradoon, and should be sized like a pelham. In most cases a horse wearing a 5½in (13.75cm) Weymouth will wear a 5¾in (14.5cm) bradoon. The Weymouth should always be worn with a curb chain or strap and a lipstrap. As you use the bottom rein, the cheek rotates pressing the bit down into the mouth and the chain into the chin groove pinching the lower jaw between the two. This gives the horse a clear signal to flex and relax the jaw and lower the head. The curb bit also gives the horse the clearest signal to stop. The upper part of the cheek should always be short so that the action is not too severe on the poll and the curb chain should stay low in the curb groove.

Shanks The longer the shank above the mouthpiece, the more leverage there is on the poll. The longer the shank below the mouthpiece, the more leverage there is on the bars of the mouth. This applies to all leverage bits. A horse or pony with a triangular shaped face needs a bit with a short upper shank that is curved outwards as the top of the cheek can easily rub or dig into the face.

Curb chains/straps These should be as heavy as possible, double link (if chain) and used with a lipstrap to encourage the chain to stay in place. The chain or curb strap should be fitted so that it comes into play when the cheek is at about a 45 degree angle.

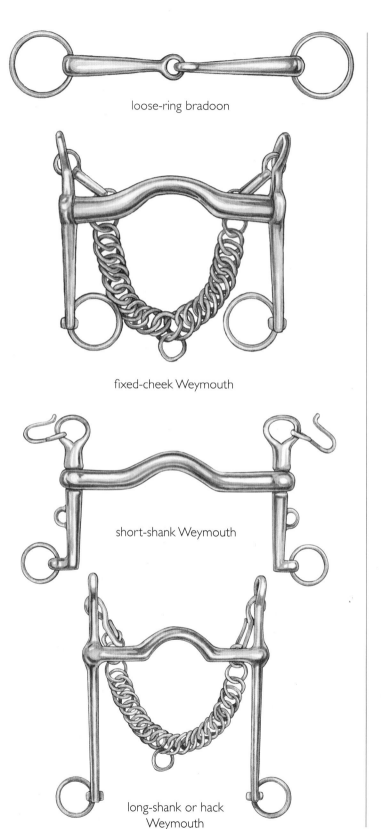

loose-ring bradoon

fixed-cheek Weymouth

short-shank Weymouth

long-shank or hack Weymouth

PORTS

Shallow ports These allow just a little tongue room. Most of the action is initially on the tongue, pressing it down into the bottom jaw and then, when the tongue is depressed, the mouthpiece finally touches the bars.

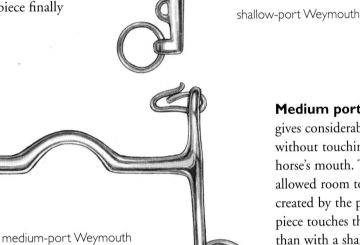

shallow-port Weymouth

medium-port Weymouth

Medium ports A medium port gives considerable tongue room without touching the roof of the horse's mouth. The tongue is allowed room to fill the space created by the port and the mouth-piece touches the bars much earlier than with a shallow-ported bit.

High ports These give the tongue plenty of room providing they are wide and not very high and narrow which would force the tongue up into a very pinched narrow space. As the rein is used, the bit rotates and then touches down onto the bars as the tongue moves up into the port. The more the bit rotates, the more the top of the port is forced into the roof of the mouth. In order to stop this action and discomfort, the horse opens his mouth slightly and tips his head over the top of the port to try to alleviate the pressure.

high-port Weymouth

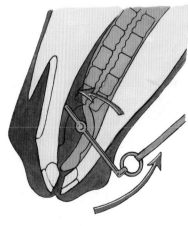

the port pressing on the roof of the mouth

PELHAMS

A pelham is really a compromise between a snaffle and a double bridle. It is a very useful bit if there is a need to ride with double reins and the horse cannot for some reason be ridden in a double bridle. If fitted with a mild mouthpiece, it is a good bit to start a less accomplished rider on the road to using two reins. To ensure the horse gets a clear signal, the pelham should always be used with two reins; the top rein simply pulls the bit back in the horse's mouth without activating the curb and the bottom rein activates the curb. You gently use each pair of reins in varying degrees to get the desired degree of control or tilt of the head. The Rugby pelham has a floating 'bradoon' ring that can be attached to a bradoon headpiece to give the appearance of a double bridle.

Single-jointed mouthpiece with a pelham cheek The action of a single-jointed curb bit really depends on how much curb rein is used. If only the top rein is pulled back, the action is not dissimilar to a jointed hanging-cheek snaffle but when the curb rein is pulled, the joint turns down in the mouth pressing into the tongue, and the cheeks are pulled in onto the horse's face. The curb chain is loose to begin with but, as the cheek rotates, the chain moves up onto the jaw bone usually taking the chain higher than the curb groove and the lower jaw is trapped in a sort of crushing triangle.

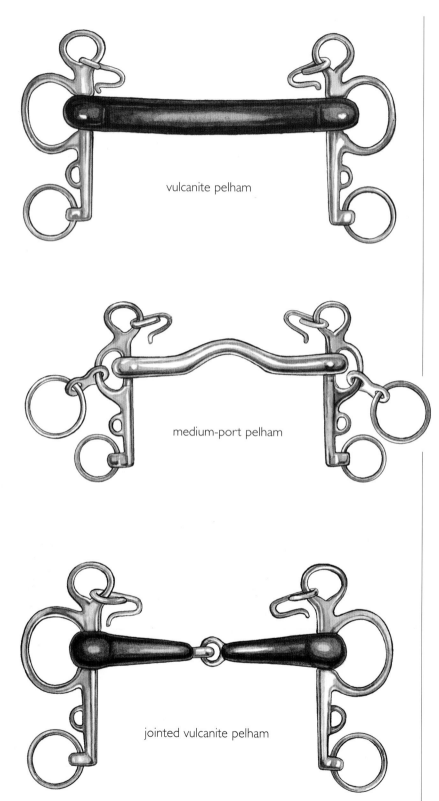

vulcanite pelham

medium-port pelham

jointed vulcanite pelham

Medium-ported mouthpiece on a pelham cheek Again, the action will depend on how much the curb rein is activated. If the bradoon rein is used, the bit works like a medium-ported snaffle with a little poll action. As you use the curb rein the mouthpiece presses down onto the tongue but the medium port allows it room to fill the space. When the tongue has filled the space, the bit moves down onto the bars of the mouth, the curb chain tightens in the curb groove and the lower jaw is held between the two. As with all curb bits this should encourage the horse to flex the jaw and lower the head.

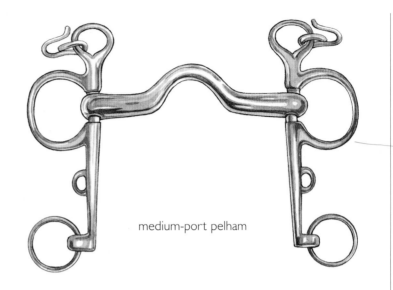

medium-port pelham

High-ported mouthpiece with a pelham cheek If the top rein, or in the case of a Liverpool bit, a mild rein setting is used, the rein only pulls the bit back in the horse's mouth acting mostly on the bars as the tongue moves into the space created by the port. But as the curb rein is used, or the lower rein settings, the cheek rotates and the top of the port pushes up into the roof of the mouth forcing the mouth to open. The tongue is pushed up into the port (a narrow port can make it very uncomfortable) and the rest of the mouthpiece presses down severely onto the bars. In order to stop this and alleviate the pressure, the horse tips his head over the top of the port and opens his mouth slightly.

high-port Liverpool

GAGS

The ordinary gag slides up and down rolled cheeks attached to the headpiece of the bridle. Leather cheeks need a lot of maintenance and are slower to release the action; nylon cheeks allow the bit to slide more freely and release the action as soon as the rein is released thus rewarding the horse much

more quickly. As the bit is able to slide up and down the cheek, leather stops below the bit prevent the bit falling too low in the horse's mouth. A gag should be used with two reins: one rein on the back of the bit ring so that the bit can be used as an ordinary bit, and one on the gag ring so the gag effect can be brought into play. By using two reins you can carefully work between the two. When the horse is going well, use the bit rein and as he begins to take a hold, reinstate the gag rein to regain more control. Constant use of the gag rein without any relief will, in most cases, deaden the horse to the constant severe pressure and pain. A gag with a snaffle mouthpiece used with a low hand on the bit rein has the same action as an ordinary snaffle. With a high hand action the bit on the gag rein slides straight up into the corners of the lips, pushing the horse's cheeks into the molars, exerting pressure on the poll and drawing the corners of the lips up towards the ears. The horse naturally wants to open his mouth and raise his head.

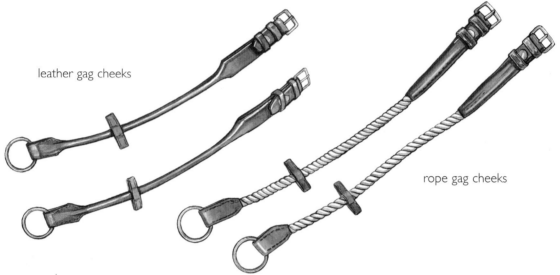

leather gag cheeks

rope gag cheeks

Single-jointed mouthpiece with a leverage cheek This type of cheek dramatically alters the action of the single joint. Depending on how far down the rein is attached on the cheek, the cheek turns the mouthpiece down and the joint pushes into the tongue pressing it down into the lower jaw. The longer the cheek the more leverage you have, therefore more pressure can be applied. As the rein is pulled back, the upper part of the cheek goes forward pulling down on the cheekpiece of the bridle and putting a lot of pressure on the poll which encourages the horse to seek relief by lowering his head and relaxing his jaw. With a four-ring bit the mouthpiece has to slide all the way round the cheek before any bit action is felt by the horse. The American gag has a similar sort of action (but not quite such a dramatic slide around the cheek before the bit comes into play) but has less rein options.

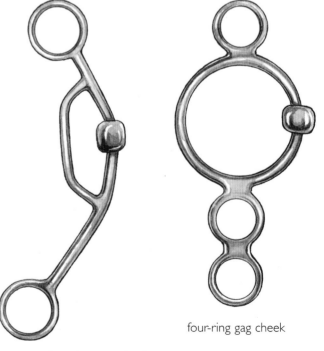

four-ring gag cheek

American gag cheek

Mullen mouthpiece with a leverage cheek This combination gives very definite downward tongue pressure. As the cheek turns, the mouthpiece of the bit pushes down evenly across the tongue pushing it down into the lower jaw. This is good for a horse with ample lower jaw capacity that needs to be ridden in something stronger than a snaffle and dislikes, or does not need, a joint or a port.

Medium port with a leverage cheek This allows considerable tongue room without touching the roof of the horse's mouth, but touches down on the bars much earlier than the previous bit. It follows the natural line inside a horse's mouth without interfering with the roof of the mouth but will put considerably more pressure onto the bars of the mouth as the tongue has been given room to rise into the port and cannot act as a buffer. It is particularly suited to a horse that needs a stronger bit and also plenty of room for the tongue. Used with two reins (as all gags should be) it acts as a ported snaffle applying a little poll pressure when the top rein only is used. If it is used with a high hand the bit will slide up into the corners of the lips. The longer the cheek the more pressure can be applied and more poll pressure is created.

French link mouthpiece with a leverage cheek Again, the action is altered when you put leverage cheeks onto a mouthpiece and use the bottom rein setting. As the rein is used, the mouthpiece turns down in the mouth and puts pressure across the tongue. The plate is turned on its edge and pushes the tongue down into the bottom jaw.

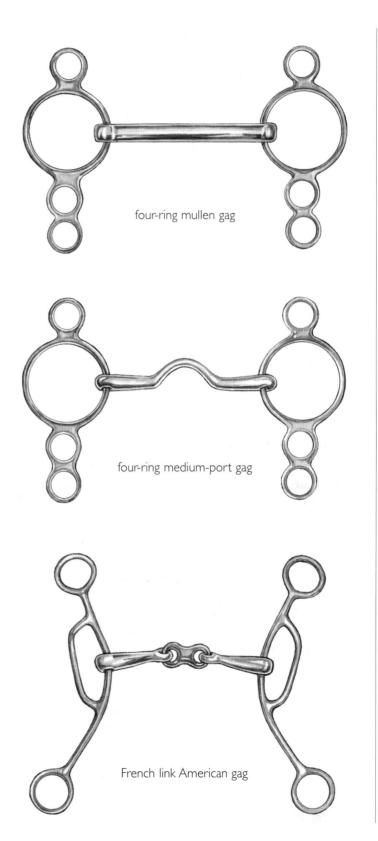

four-ring mullen gag

four-ring medium-port gag

French link American gag

Dr. Bristol mouthpiece with a leverage cheek The top rein setting will always give a very similar action to a snaffle bit but the farther down the leverage rein settings you go the more poll action you create. The mouthpiece of this bit, if used with a lower rein setting, will push down into the horse's mouth lying the plate flat on the tongue as opposed to sticking into the tongue as happens when this mouthpiece is on a snaffle cheek.

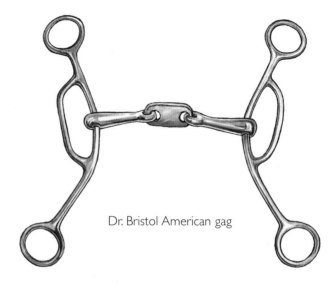

Dr. Bristol American gag

CARRIAGE BITS

Most carriage bits have multiple settings ranging from very mild to extremely severe. This is because when the horse is harnessed to a carriage, you are committed to going forward at a controlled pace. Unlike a riding horse, a carriage horse cannot spin round, go into a driveway, or shy into a ditch without dire consequences for himself and the carriage and whip (driver). So, by having several options you have the choice in a potentially difficult situation of using a stronger rein setting for a short while until the excitement has passed or to get you home safely so you can revue the situation.

Driving bits fall into five categories or cheek types, with varying mouthpieces. The Wilson snaffle, the Liverpool, the Buxton, the military reversible and the butterfly or post bit.

The Liverpool This is the most widely used driving bit. It comes in a variety of different mouthpieces, with fixed or sliding cheeks, and in several cheek lengths, with a two- or three-slot cheek, (providing either one rein slot or two to buckle the reins into below the mouth piece). The curb chain should be flat and untwisted and come into action when the cheek is at a 45 degree angle. If using a riding bridle curb chain, the back ring or fly link that would normally carry a lipstrap should be cut off.

There are four rein attachment positions on the bit.

1. Plain cheek The rein simply pulls the bit back and up in the mouth and does not engage the curb chain.

2. Rough cheek The rein pulls the bit back and engages a little curb action.

3. Middle bar The rein pulls the bit down in the mouth engaging the curb and pinching the tongue and lower jaw between the mouthpiece and the curb chain. It also exerts a certain amount of poll pressure.

4. Bottom bar This is the most severe rein position and is really only a last resort in a crisis. When the rein is applied it exerts maximum poll and curb pressure.

Liverpool rein settings

1
2
3
4

If the Liverpool is used with a pair of horses the bit must either be a fixed cheek or used only on the rough cheek position as the inside rein comes across from the opposite horse's pad at an angle, the cheek swivels and pinches the horse's top lip.

The Wilson snaffle This is a snaffle with two extra floating rings that the cheekpieces are attached to. Normally the reins are buckled through both rings. Buckling through the fixed rings alone makes it very severe, crushing the horse's face between the cheekpiece rings. When harnessing up, take care that the horse does not turn the bit over in his mouth before you have buckled up the reins or you might find that you are driving with the bit upside down. The Wilson snaffle can have flat or wire cheeks but does not have the rein options of some of the other driving bits.

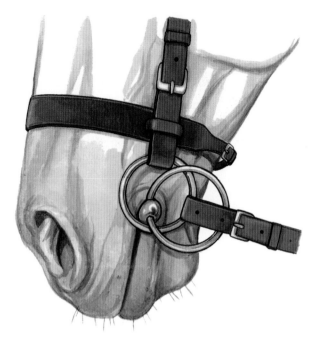

Wilson snaffle with reins buckled

The military reversible or elbow The cheek is angled back to ensure the horse cannot get hold of it with his teeth and to ensure it does not pinch the top lip because the inner reins of a pair always pull the inner cheek at an angle. A very useful pairs bit, it comes in a variety of mouthpieces. The Ashleigh pattern has the most rein options. The bit in a Barmouth or Port is reversible; it can have a smooth mouthpiece on one side and a rough mouthpiece on the other; the curb chain can be flipped over so that the bit can be used on either side. Other mouthpieces such as the French link or Dr. Bristol cannot be reversed.

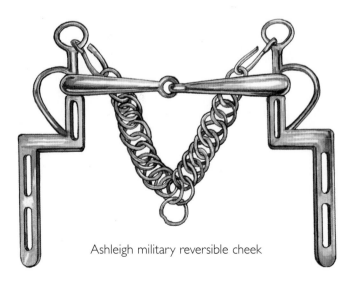

Ashleigh military reversible cheek

The Buxton This is very much a coaching bit mainly used with Private Drags or with very smart owner-driven pairs vehicles. Some bits can be very ornate with angled cheeks and a bottom bar. There are several different patterns, some with more rein options than others.

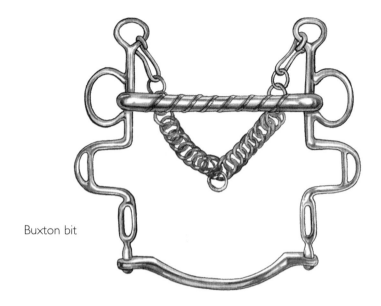

Buxton bit

The butterfly or post bit The smaller version of this bit is called a butterfly and is suited to the small pony head, both for pairs and singles. Two rein options give it a very neat appearance for the smaller head. The larger versions are normally called post bits and suit a larger head. They can have two or three rein options. Both come in a variety of mouthpieces.

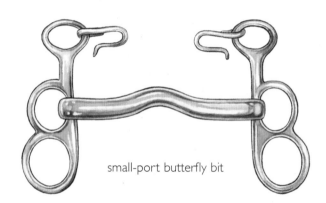

small-port butterfly bit

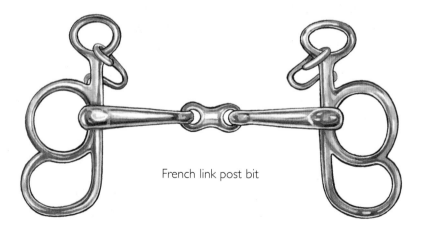

French link post bit

Chapter 10

How to Fit Different Bits

To fit a bit correctly, the bit should be on a bridle with the noseband undone.

Jointed eggbutt snaffle To check the correct height in the mouth, the bit should fit snugly into the corners of the lips, just wrinkling the corners without pulling the face up. If you pull down lightly on the rings the bit should not leave a gap between it and the corners of the mouth. To get the width right, stand in front of your horse and take a bit ring in each hand. Pull the bit rings so the bit is straight in the mouth, you should just be able to place one finger sideways between the bit ring and the horse's lip on each side of the mouth. If the bit is too wide the joint will hang too low in the mouth and could interfere with the horse's front teeth or hang out of the side of the mouth in an unsightly fashion. If the bit is very wide it will slide from side to side in the mouth.

Jointed loose-ring snaffle Check the height in the mouth in the same way as with an eggbut snaffle but loose-ring bits should be fitted slightly wider to prevent pinching. There should be ¼in (6mm) gap each side of the horse's face. If the bit is too narrow, as the cheek slides through the ring in the mouthpiece there is a danger that the lips can be drawn into the gap and pinched.

Mullen snaffle The fitting principles of the

jointed eggbut snaffle also apply here: there should be a finger's width on each side of the mouth or, with a loose-ring mullen, ¼in (6mm) space either side of the mouth. The height is correct when the bit slightly wrinkles the corners of the lips and, again, you should not be able to pull the bit away from the corners of the mouth. It is important not to have a mullen bit too wide as it can slide from side to side in the mouth. Very lightweight mullen or straight bar bits with small rings are designed to be used with in-hand bridles because it is very easy for the bit to be turned over in the mouth. The in-hand bridle has the cheekpiece secured by the noseband so the fitting is much more stable.

Cheeked and D ring snaffles The same basic fitting principles apply but you may find some horses are more comfortable with a little more width so that the cheek fits the face without rubbing. Cheeked snaffles should always be secured to the bridle cheek by a small leather keeper to help to keep the bit in the correct position in the mouth and, in the case of the Fulmer snaffle, to stop the cheekpieces from hanging down loosely.

Pelhams and Kimblewicks Any pelham or Kimblewick with a sliding cheek has the potential to pinch the corners of the lips. When buying, make sure that the cheeks move freely and are smoothly constructed. To fit, there must be ¼in

(6mm) gap on each side of the horse's face and, again, the bit should fit snugly into the corners of the lips. Too wide a bit will move from side to side in the mouth and interfere with the action. With a particularly sensitive horse, rubber bit guards can be fitted to each side of the bit though these are not permitted in all disciplines.

Gags With the three types of gag, the Continental or four-ring, the American and the English, the same fitting principles apply: if the gag is an eggbut or loose ring, it will fit like a snaffle. A gag, whatever the type, should be used with two reins so that the gag action is only used when you need it.

Double bridle The bradoon should be fitted as a snaffle, above not below the Weymouth. The Weymouth should lie just below the bradoon. Generally speaking, for the most comfortable fit, the bradoon should be ¼in (6mm) wider than the Weymouth, i.e. a 5½in (13.75cm) Weymouth would go with a 5¾in (14.5cm) bradoon. It is generally accepted that a loose-ring bradoon is used with a sliding-cheek Weymouth and an eggbut bradoon is used with a fixed-cheek Weymouth, although you often see different combinations working very well. The curb chain action should be felt when the cheek of the Weymouth is at a 45 degree angle. The curb chain must lie flat in the curb groove and always be accompanied by a lip-strap. For a very sensitive horse, a leather curb strap or a leather-covered jelly curb chain protector may be the answer.

The bitless bridle A bitless bridle needs to be positioned with great care, it must not interfere with the horse's breathing so must lie on the nose bone above the nasal cartilage but not be fitted so high that it interferes with and rubs the projecting cheek bone.

Chapter 11

Combination Hackamore Bridles

Norton or Citation This bridle is made up of two mouthpieces, one a loose-ring, thin wire, jointed overcheck, the other a loose-ring jointed bradoon. The cheek pieces of the bridle attach to the rings of the overcheck. The reins attach to the rings of the bradoon. Around the mouthpiece of the overcheck are two metal fixtures that carry a nosepiece. This is a severe bridle combining very thin snaffle mouth-pieces with nose and poll pressure. As the reins are used, the cheeks of the overcheck are pushed into the horse's face and the joint is forced up into the roof of the mouth. The more the bit pulls back in the mouth the more nose and corner of lip pressure is brought to bear.

Newmarket This usually consists of a Wilson snaffle with a mullen or jointed mouthpiece with a leather nosepiece attached to the floating ring and supported by small straps connected to the cheekpiece of the bridle. This bridle is used with two reins so that when the snaffle rein is used, the bit acts

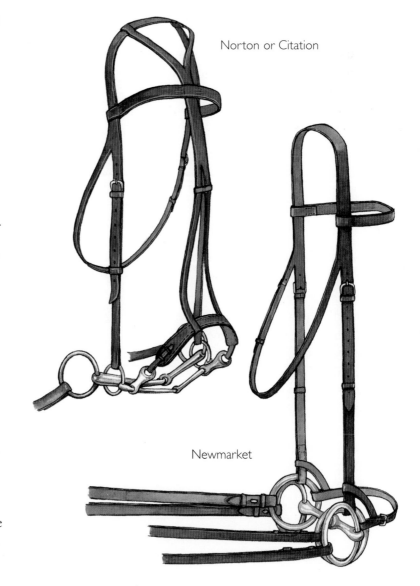

Norton or Citation

Newmarket

as a snaffle with the added severity of the floating rings pushing in on the sides of the horse's face. This happens mainly with the jointed snaffle and not with the mullen. When the rein attached to the floating ring is used, more pressure is transferred to the nose. In a less severe form the nosepiece is attached to an ordinary snaffle so that, with an adjustment to the nosepiece, you can relieve a lot of pressure on the mouth. The nosepiece can be adjusted on both types so that the pressure can be transferred from the mouth to the nose or a combination of both in differing degrees.

Rockwell The Rockwell uses the same type of nosepiece as the Citation but has only one loose-ring jointed snaffle. The nosepiece fits onto the bit in the same way. As the rein is applied, the bit acts like a snaffle, i.e. the more the bit pulls back in the mouth, nose and poll pressure are brought to bear.

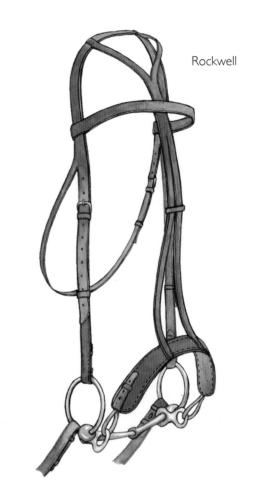

Rockwell

Combination nose bridle and bit
This is often an American gag with a hackamore front attached which has the combined effect of a gag and strong nose pressure. The bridle must be of good quality as badly made versions tend to have the nosepiece far too long causing the nosepiece to drop too far down the nose giving severe discomfort.

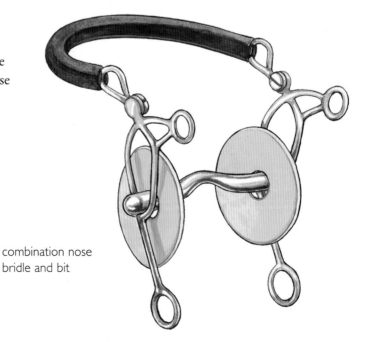

combination nose bridle and bit

Scawbrigg bridle A simple form of a bitless bridle, the Scawbrigg is made of a padded nosepiece usually lined with chamois leather or sheepskin. The nosepiece is supported by a small piece of leather attached to the cheek of the bridle. The back is a wide padded piece resting on the horse's jaw bones passing through the rings of the nosepiece to become reins. There should be a supporting strap fastening at the back passing through a loop on the chin piece to stop the noseband twisting round. It should be fitted three or four finger widths above the nostrils so the action does not interfere with the horse's breathing. This noseband can also be used in conjunction with a bit: the bit is attached to a bradoon headpiece and a separate pair of reins is used for both the nose-piece and the bit.

Scrawbrigg bridle

In Conclusion

I am not putting myself forward as a leading authority on bits and bitting and I don't think I have really said anything that hasn't been said before and by far more learned people than I. There are things that I have intentionally left out because I feel it is important to write about only those things you have experienced first hand or had thoroughly explained to you.

When working in the saddlery business, I always thought that it would have made things so much easier if I could have shown pictures of the bit that I was trying to describe or to be able to show certain parts of the mouth. In writing this book I hope I have done that and made things clearer. There is no denying that bitting is a complex subject but I really think that with a little thought it can be far easier. I have always found technical books very wordy and my aim was to try to put things into a simpler and more understandable form.

PART II

A PICTORIAL GUIDE TO BITS

The following pages are example pictures of bits set into families.
It is possible, within reason, to match many mouthpieces with different
cheeks. So the illustrated bits can be converted into very many more
combinations. Some of the bits are extremely severe and are not
recommended but are shown merely as examples of type. Throughout
this section, vulcanite/rubber = vulcanite or rubber.

Snaffles

standard eggbutt

thick-mouth eggbutt

standard loose ring

thick-mouth loose ring

French link eggbutt

French link loose ring

Snaffles

mullen eggbutt

mullen loose ring

low-port loose ring

medium-port eggbutt

medium-port loose ring

Barmouth (straight bar) loose ring

Snaffles

vulcanite / rubber mullen loose ring

vulcanite / rubber jointed eggbutt

vulcanite / rubber French link loose ring

vulcanite / rubber jointed loose ring

vulcanite / rubber mullen eggbutt

Salisbury French link

Snaffles

twisted loose ring   Scorrier (Cornish)

Dr. Bristol eggbutt   Dr. Bristol loose ring

Dick Christian   Magenis

Snaffles

Waterford loose ring

copper roller Waterford loose ring

Waterford eggbutt (kangeroo)

copper windsucker loose ring

cherry roller

Nagbut loose ring

Snaffles

Barmouth figure 8 (rotating)   jointed beval

copper roller Waterford beval   Captain Sandy

twisted swivel

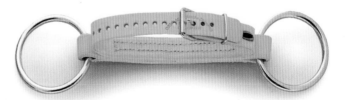

Sprenger leather

Snaffles

two-mouth W   three-mouth W

jointed loose-ring copper roller   thick-mouth Dick Christian

twisted wire

antilugging

double twisted jointed wire

Snaffles

curb chain

Norton perfection (Citation)

Rockwell

bike chain

arch crescendo

jointed crescendo

Hanoverian eggbutt

Cheeked snaffles

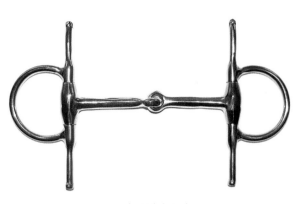

eggbutt jointed

ball cheek french link

ball cheek vulcanite / rubber jointed

ball cheek Dr. Bristol

ball cheek with players

ball cheek twisted

Cheeked snaffles

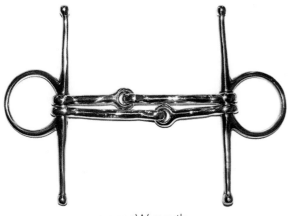

copper W mouth

eggbutt French link

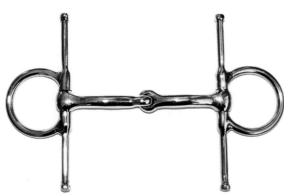

ball cheek jointed

ball cheek vulcanite / rubber mullen

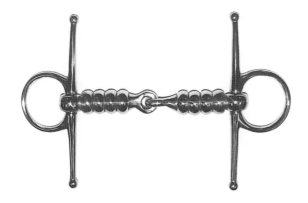

ball cheek cherry roller

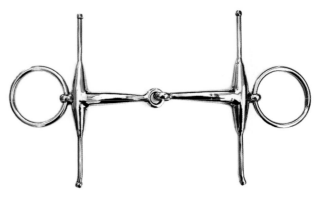

Fulmer

Cheeked snaffles

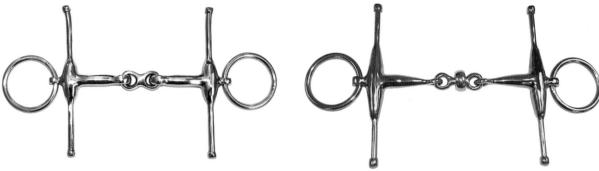

French link Fulmer

Fulmer link copper ball

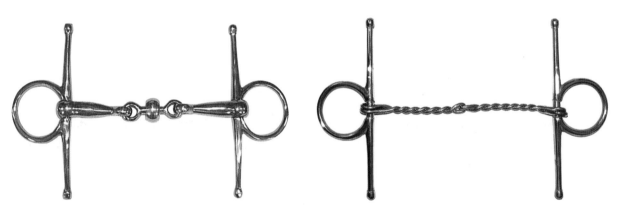

ball cheek copper ball

ball cheek copper twisted wire

ball cheek copper double twisted wire

Waterford

Cheeked snaffles

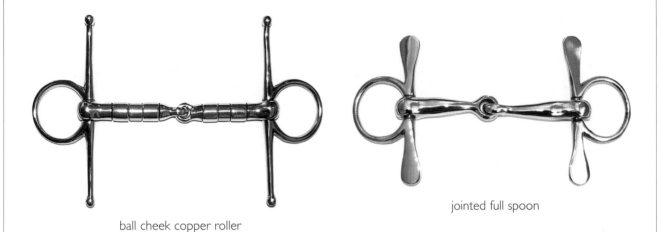

ball cheek copper roller

jointed full spoon

half-spoon jointed

half-spoon mullen

half-spoon Dr. Bristol

half-spoon vulcanite/rubber jointed

Cheeked snaffles

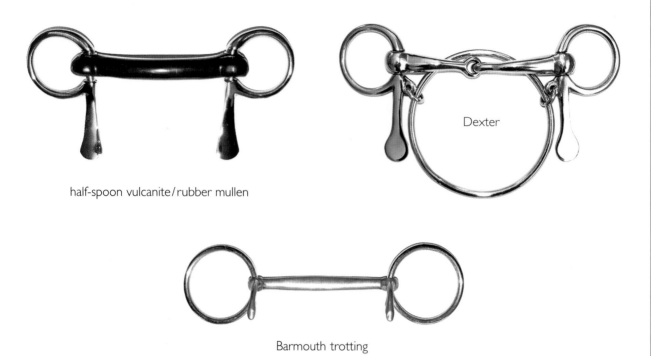

half-spoon vulcanite/rubber mullen

Dexter

Barmouth trotting

Hanging-cheek snaffles

mullen

jointed

French link

Hanging-cheek snaffles

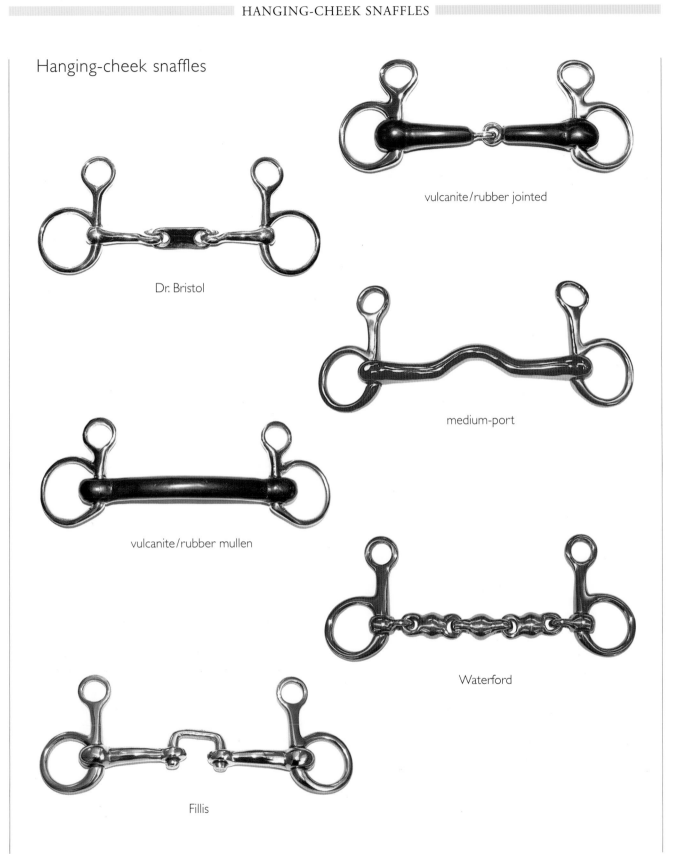

vulcanite/rubber jointed

Dr. Bristol

medium-port

vulcanite/rubber mullen

Waterford

Fillis

Hanging-cheek snaffles

Fillis with players

jointed copper roller

D cheek snaffles

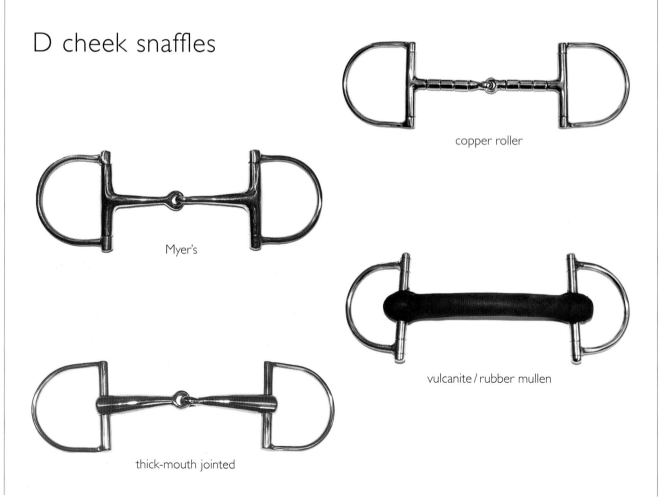

copper roller

Myer's

vulcanite / rubber mullen

thick-mouth jointed

D cheek snaffles

Waterford

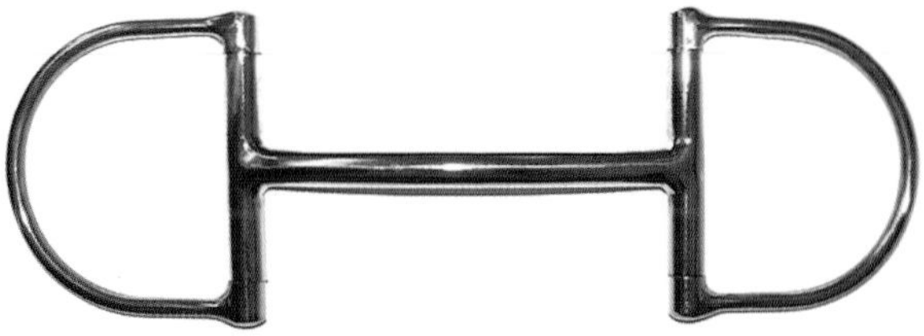

mullen

twisted

Waterford copper roller

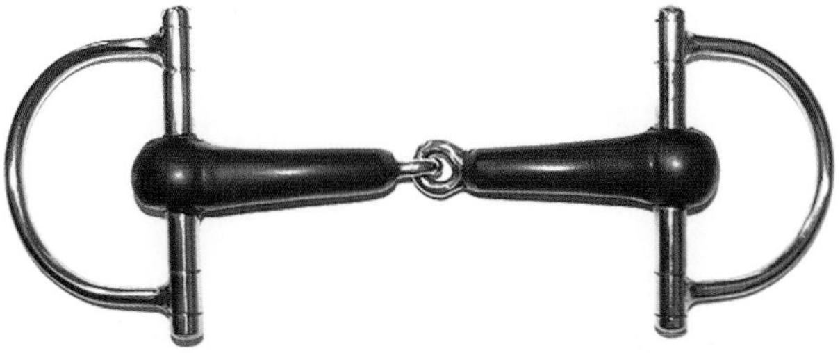

vulcanite / rubber jointed

In-hand/breaking

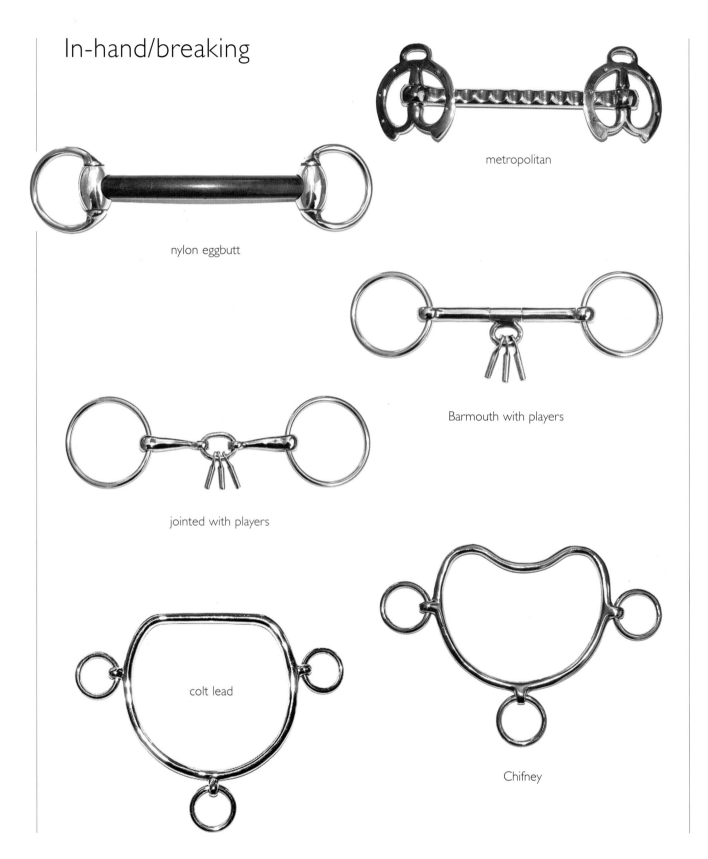

metropolitan

nylon eggbutt

Barmouth with players

jointed with players

colt lead

Chifney

In-hand/breaking

mullen-mouth nylon loose ring

Tattersal ring
with players

Pelhams

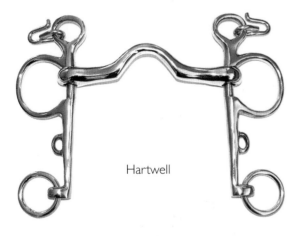

Hartwell

jointed copper

high-port

French link

Pelhams

rubber loller

vulcanite / rubber mullen

egglink (curved cheek)

vulcanite / rubber jointed

Pelhams

copper jointed

bike chain

copper cherry roller jointed

Coscoquero

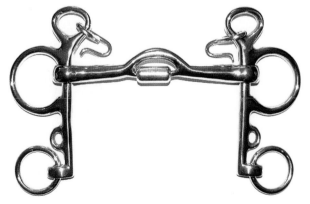

Coscoquero large cricket

Pelhams

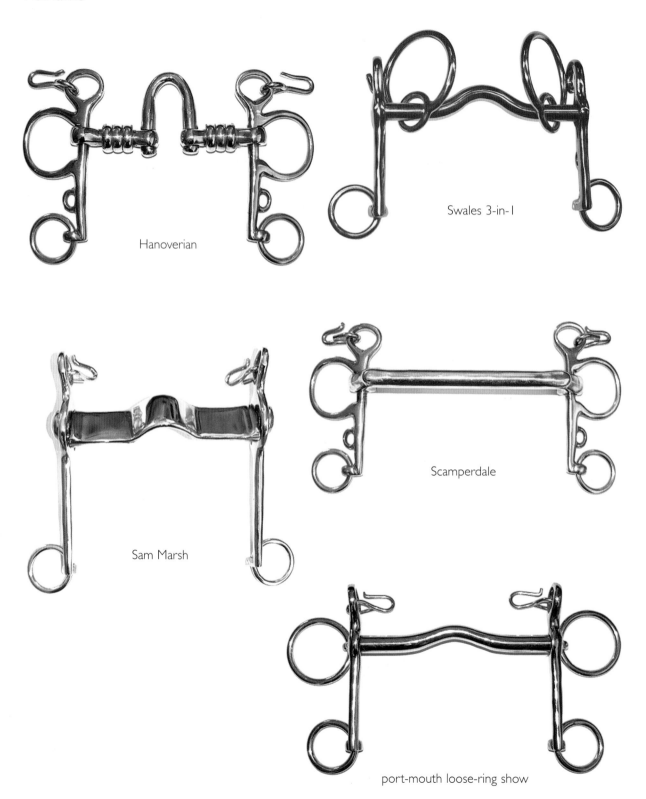

Hanoverian

Swales 3-in-1

Sam Marsh

Scamperdale

port-mouth loose-ring show

Pelhams

fixed-cheek Hanoverian

fixed-port Hanoverian pelham

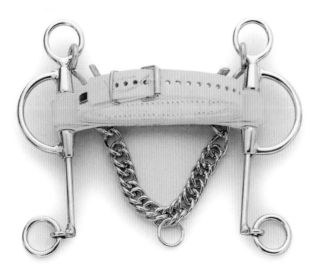

Sprenger leather

Rugby pelhams

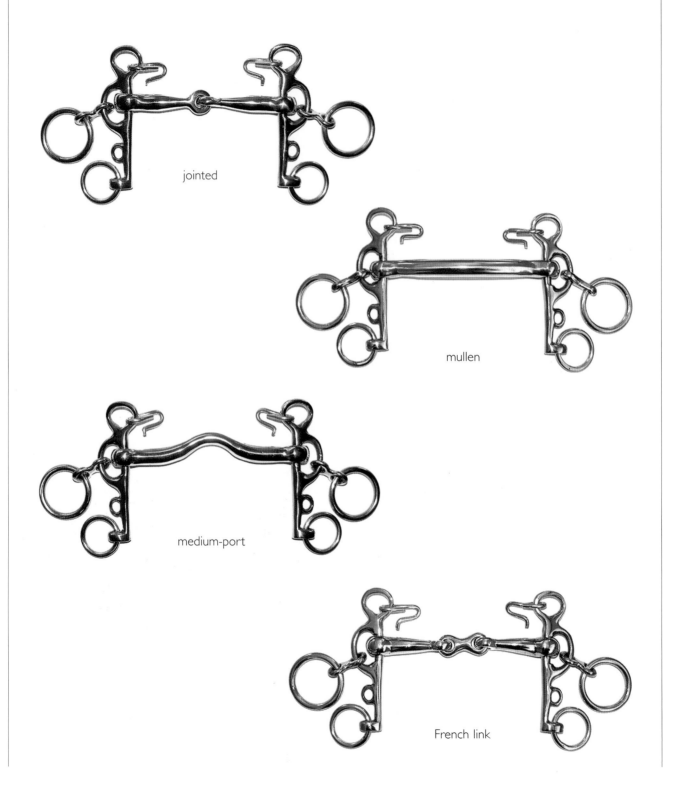

jointed

mullen

medium-port

French link

Rugby pelhams

Hartwell

vulcanite/rubber mullen

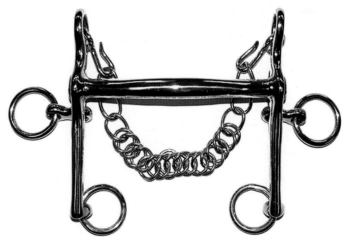

fixed-cheek mullen

Kimblewick pelhams

mullen slotted

jointed slotted

square-port Hanoverian

vulcanite / rubber

vulcanite / rubber slotted

medium-port slotted

Globe pelhams

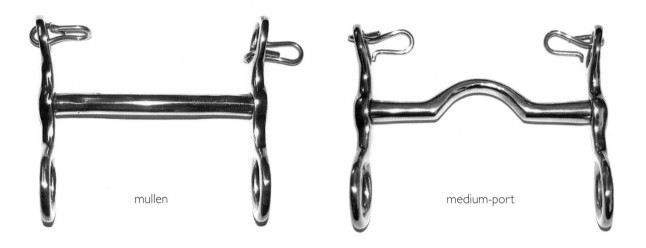

mullen

medium-port

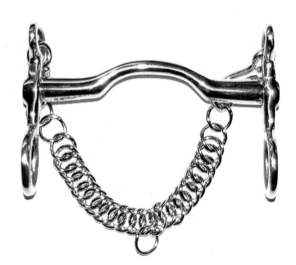

medium-wide-port

Weymouths

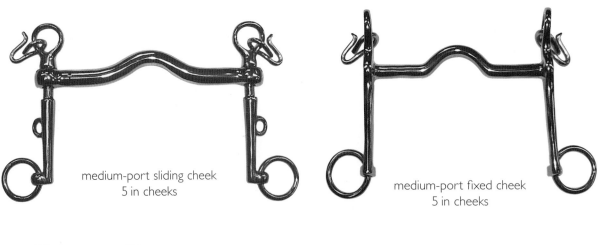

medium-port sliding cheek
5 in cheeks

medium-port fixed cheek
5 in cheeks

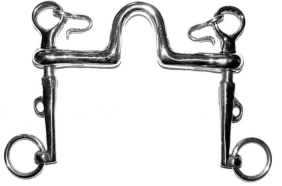

high-port sliding cheek

medium-port Tom Thumb
4 in cheeks

low-port hack fixed cheek
6 in cheeks

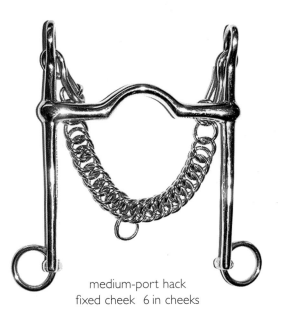

medium-port hack
fixed cheek 6 in cheeks

Weymouths

medium-wide-port fixed cheek

vulcanite / rubber mullen

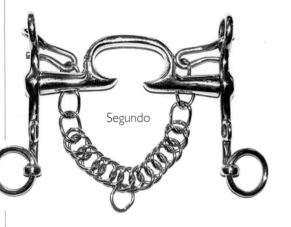

Segundo

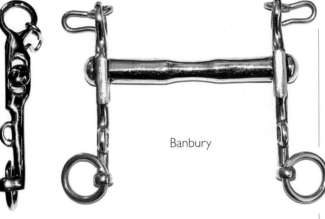

Banbury

Mors L'hotte

mullen

Sprenger Weymouths

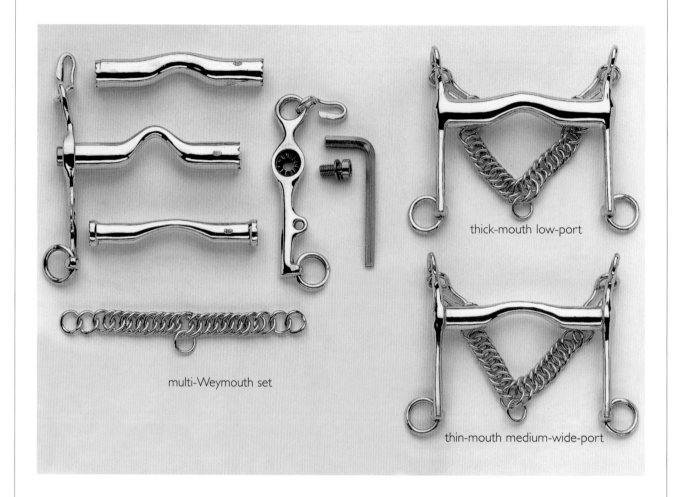

multi-Weymouth set

thick-mouth low-port

thin-mouth medium-wide-port

thick-mouth medium-port

Mors L' hotte

Sprenger Weymouths

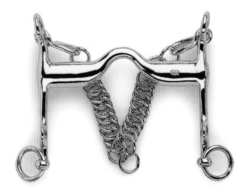

thick-mouth high-port

medium-mouth high-port

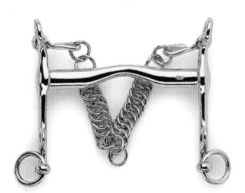

medium-mouth low-port

thick-mouth low-port swan cheek

thick-mouth high-port swan cheek

Bradoons

jointed eggbutt

jointed loose ring

French link loose ring

jointed twisted

Gag snaffles

standard jointed Cheltenham

vulcanite/rubber jointed Cheltenham

Gag snaffles

mullen Cheltenham

vulcanite/rubber mullen Cheltenham

Salisbury

twisted Cheltenham

twisted Barry

French link Cheltenham

Duncan

cherry roller Cheltenham

Gag snaffles

jointed copper ball Balding

flexible rubber mullen Balding

jointed cherry roller Balding

vulcanite/rubber jointed Balding

jointed twisted Balding

French link Balding

Gag snaffles

jointed Balding   mullen Balding

jointed half Balding   twisted jointed half Balding

French link half Balding   half-twisted jointed half Balding

Gag snaffles

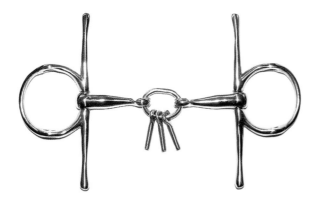

jointed Nelson with players

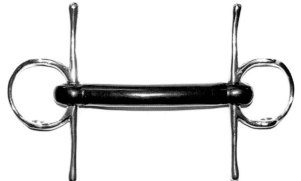

vulcanite/rubber mullen Nelson

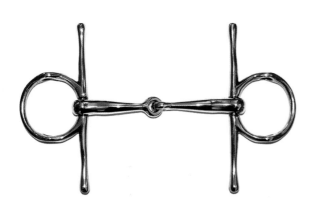

jointed Nelson

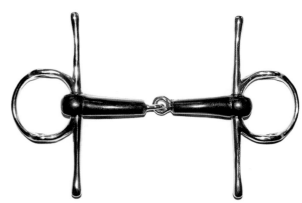

vulcanite/rubber jointed Nelson

Dr. Bristol Balding

Hitchcock

Gag snaffles

double twisted copper wire Balding

Barry

rubber jointed French link Balding

Polo gag snaffles

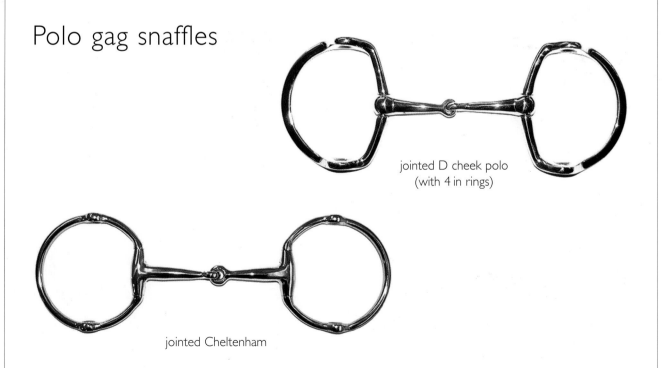

jointed D cheek polo
(with 4 in rings)

jointed Cheltenham

Polo gag snaffles

thick-mouth Balding

thick-mouth copper Balding

jointed Balding

twisted Cheltenham

Polo gag snaffles

vulcanite / rubber mullen Balding

Dr. Bristol Balding

twisted Balding

single twisted Barry

American gags

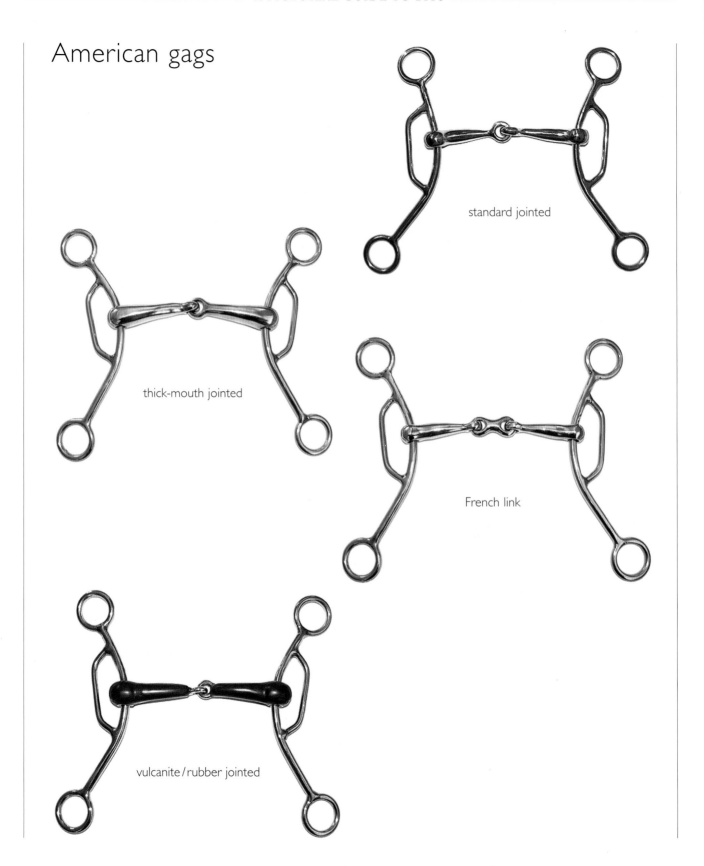

standard jointed

thick-mouth jointed

French link

vulcanite / rubber jointed

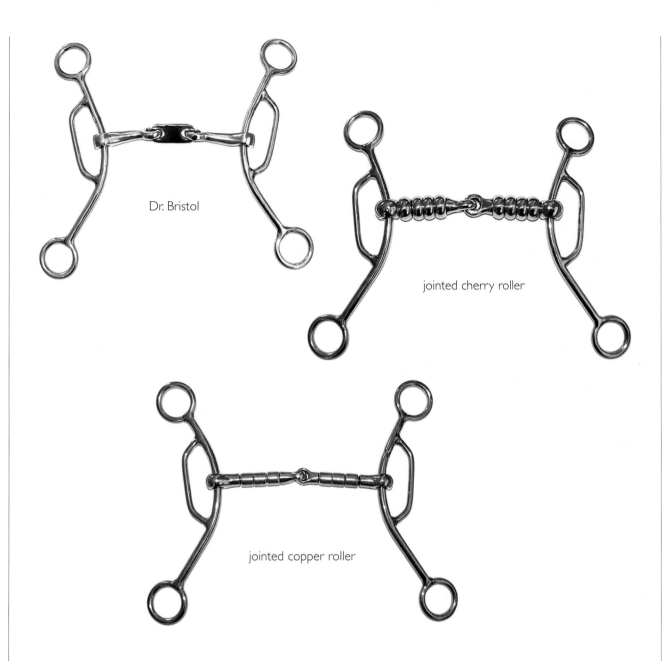

Dr. Bristol

jointed cherry roller

jointed copper roller

Four-ring / continental gag

There is also a three-ring cheek available but to show both three- and four-ring cheeks would mean repeating the same mouthpieces.

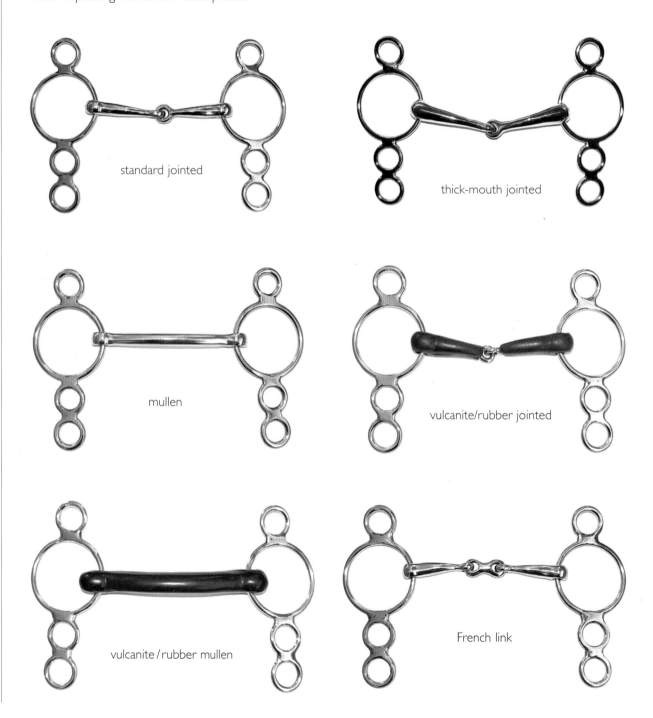

standard jointed

thick-mouth jointed

mullen

vulcanite/rubber jointed

vulcanite / rubber mullen

French link

Four-ring/continental gag

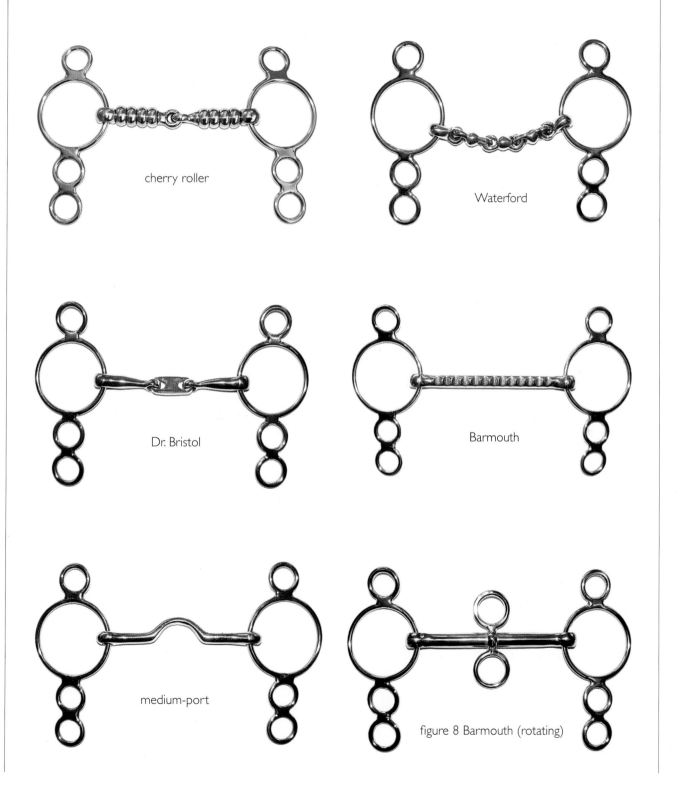

cherry roller

Waterford

Dr. Bristol

Barmouth

medium-port

figure 8 Barmouth (rotating)

Carriage (Wilsons)

vulcanite / rubber jointed   rubber mullen

jointed   mullen

twisted jointed

Carriage (Wilsons)

French link   horseshoe

Carriage (Liverpools)

All Liverpool bits come with a two-slot cheek as well as the three-slot cheek as shown.

jointed

Barmouth crown pattern

mullen

Carriage (Liverpools)

mullen copper mouth

arch

medium-port

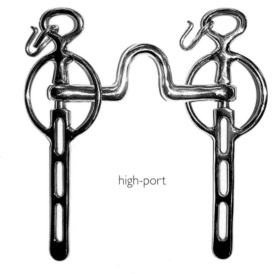

high-port

high-port fixed cheek

thick-mouth jointed

Carriage (Liverpools)

vulcanite / rubber
jointed

vulcanite / rubber mullen bottom bar

French link
bottom bar

Coscoquero

high-port
bottom bar

French link

Carriage (Liverpools)

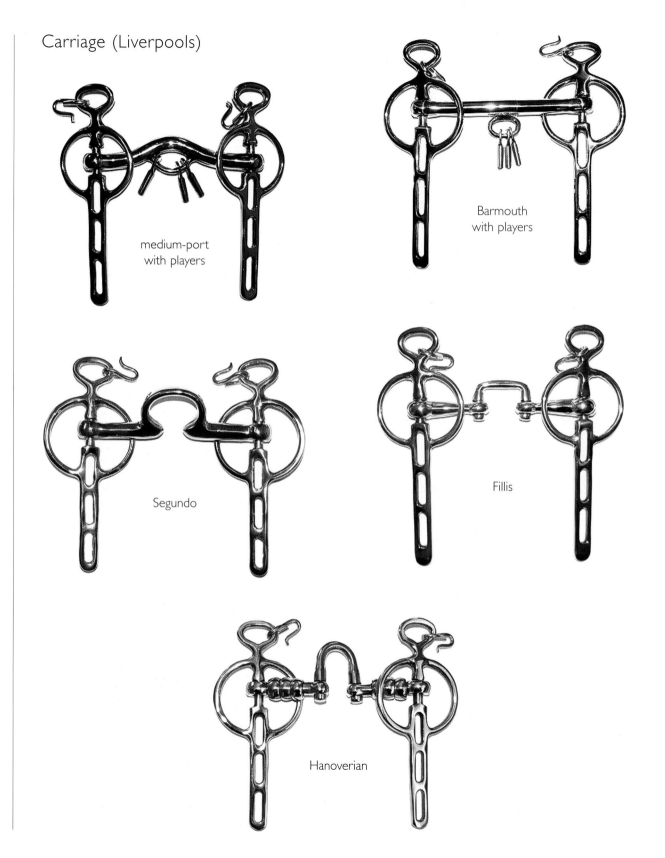

medium-port
with players

Barmouth
with players

Segundo

Fillis

Hanoverian

Carriage (Liverpools)

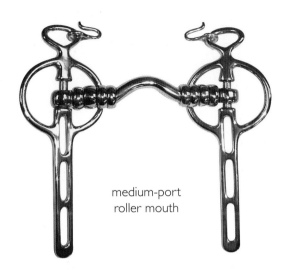

medium-port
roller mouth

straight bar cherry roller

Carriage (Swales / Buxtons)

medium-port
Liverpool Swales

Barmouth with
bottom bar Swales

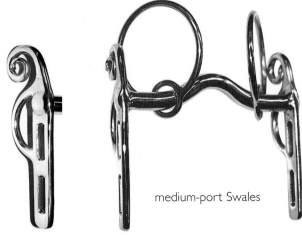

medium-port Swales

Carriage (Swales/Buxtons)

Barmouth Buxton

Hanoverian Buxton

Carriage (military style)

vulcanite jointed

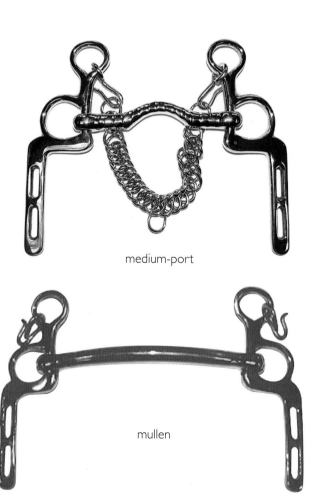

medium-port

mullen

Carriage (military style)

high-port

vulcanite mullen

jointed Ashleigh

Barmouth bottom bar
Ashleigh

Carriage (butterfly)

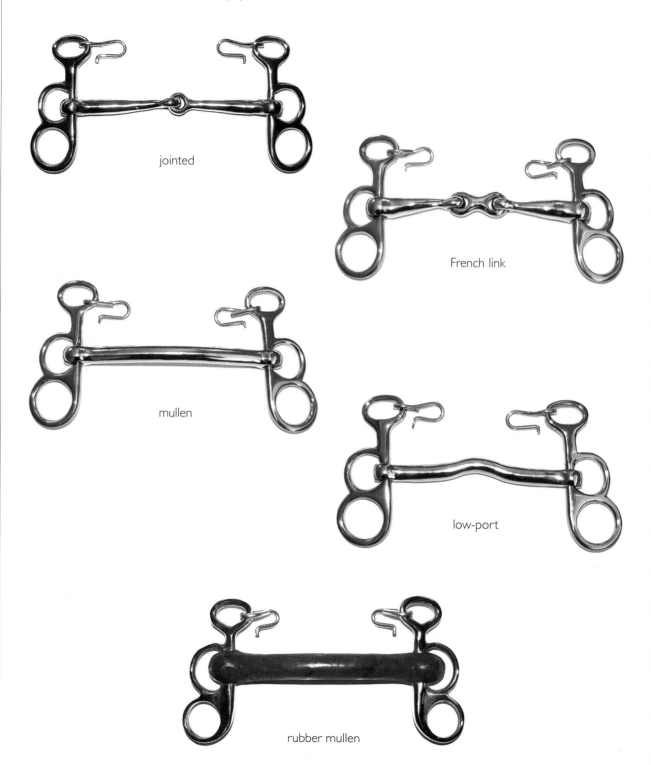

jointed

French link

mullen

low-port

rubber mullen

Carriage (post)

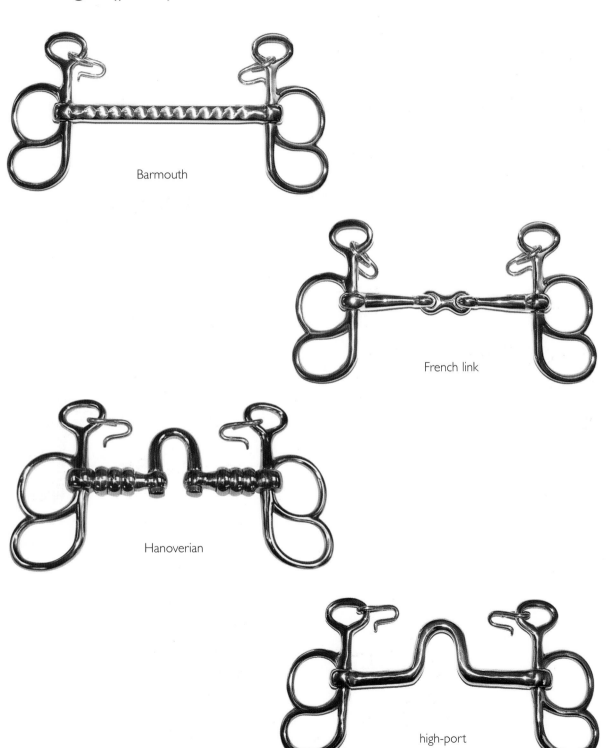

Barmouth

French link

Hanoverian

high-port

Overchecks/grids

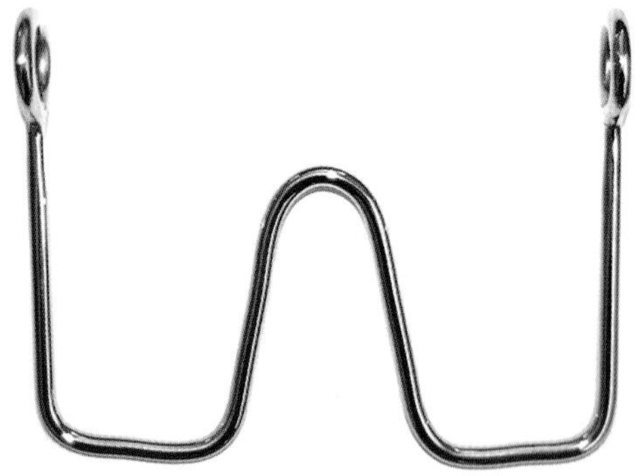

W tongue grid

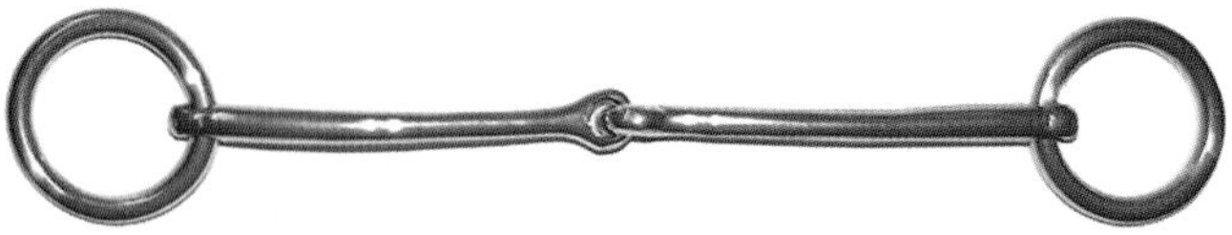

jointed overcheck

twisted jointed overcheck

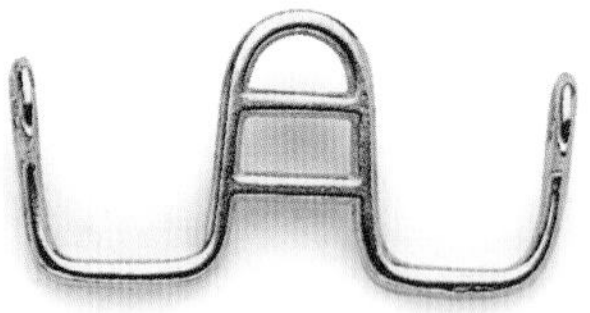

grid overcheck

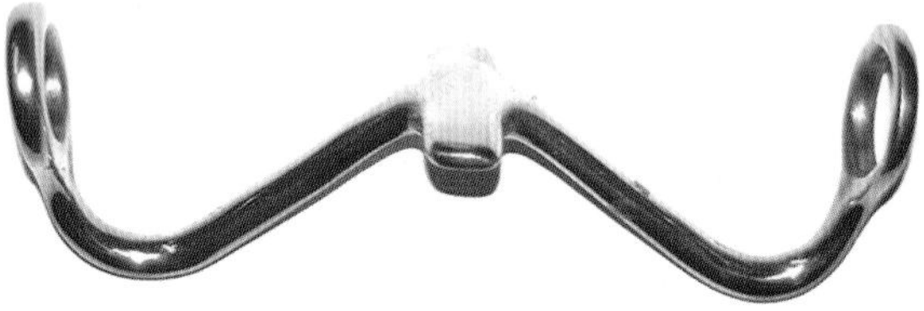

Burch overcheck

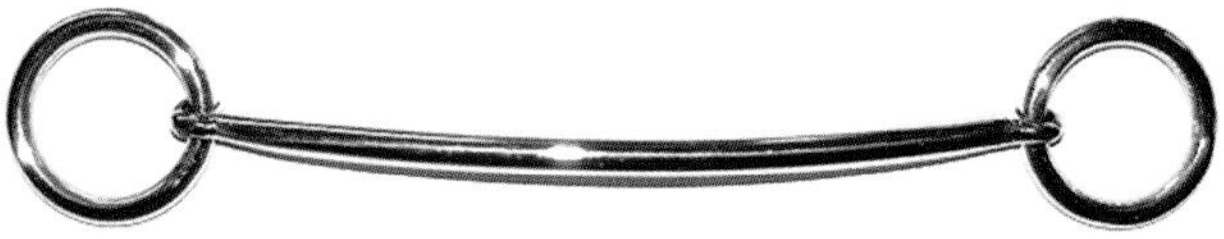

mullen overcheck

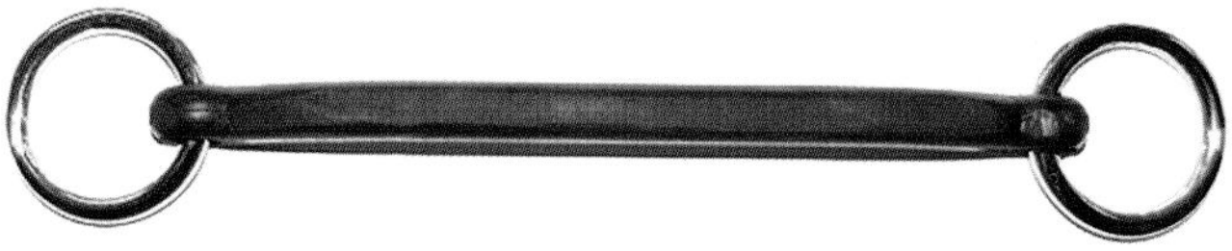

rubber mullen overcheck

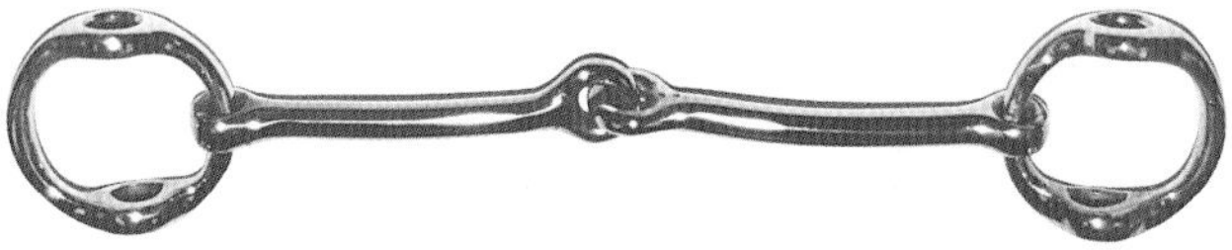

jointed gag overcheck

Nathe

These German-made bits were the first real alternatives to rubber bits. The soft, flexible mouth-pieces do not have the bulkiness usually associated with rubber bits. Nathe bits encourage a horse to move towards, and accept the feel of, the bit.

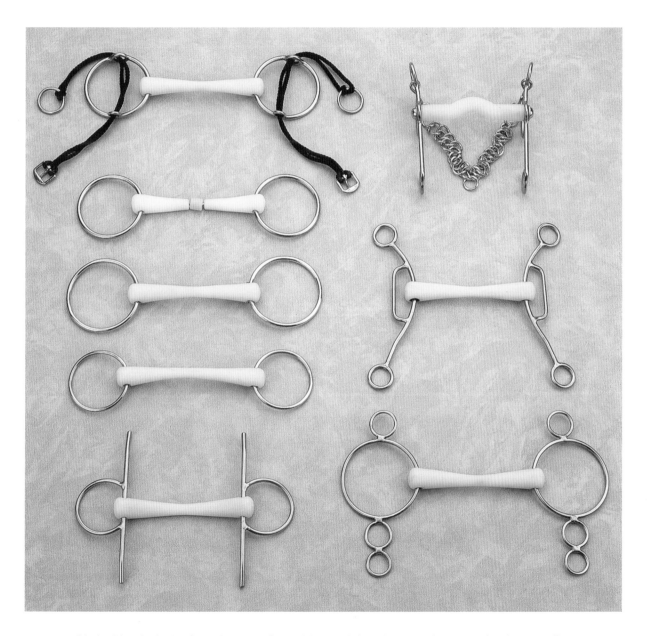

Nathe bits, clockwise from the top left: gag; Liverpool; American gag; 4-ring gag; full cheek snaffle; small ring snaffle; large ring snaffle; jointed snaffle

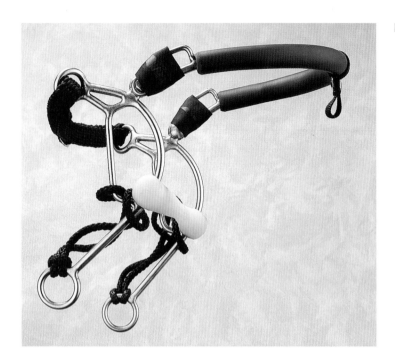

Nathe combination hackamore

KK bits

KK bits were designed by the famous German sculptor Ulrich Conrad. As well as being an equestrian sculptor, he is a horse lover and enthusiastic rider. For more than two decades he has studied the effects of different bits on horses' mouths and carried out extensive tests before creating the optimal shapes of the KK bits. They are specially designed to follow the contours of the horse's mouth, alleviating a lot of tongue pressure.

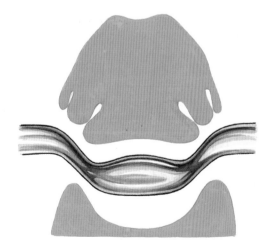

correction bit in the mouth

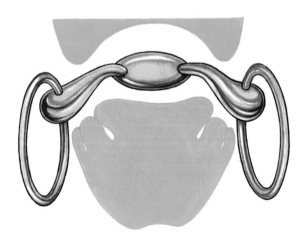

training bit in the mouth

KK bits

training

schooling

correction

loose-ring snaffle

loose-ring double-jointed snaffle

KK bits

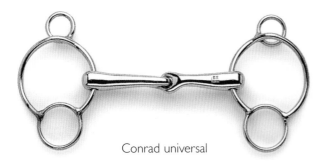

Conrad universal

Conrad universal double jointed

Conrad pelham

Conrad jumping bit

dressage Weymouth

KK carriage bits

KK carriage bits, clockwise from the top left: Conrad three-slot Liverpool;
Conrad Ashleigh military reversible; Conrad two-slot Liverpool; Conrad butterfly;

Happy Mouth bits

The Happy Mouth range of bits was invented to meet a demand for a softer more comfortable alternative to cold metal. The range offers a wide choice of different bits to suit various mouth shapes and degrees of severity. The bits imported into this country have two inner constructions but different designs are available overseas.

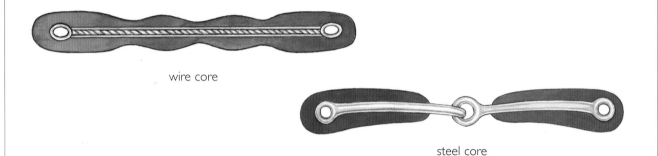

wire core

steel core

Happy Mouth wire core

D ring straight-bar snaffle

eggbutt straight-bar snaffle

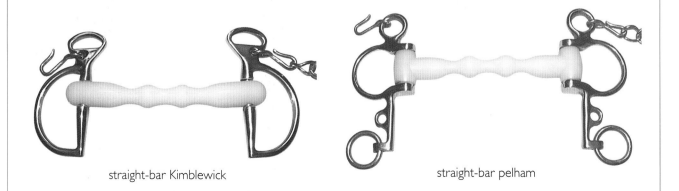

straight-bar Kimblewick

straight-bar pelham

Happy Mouth wire core

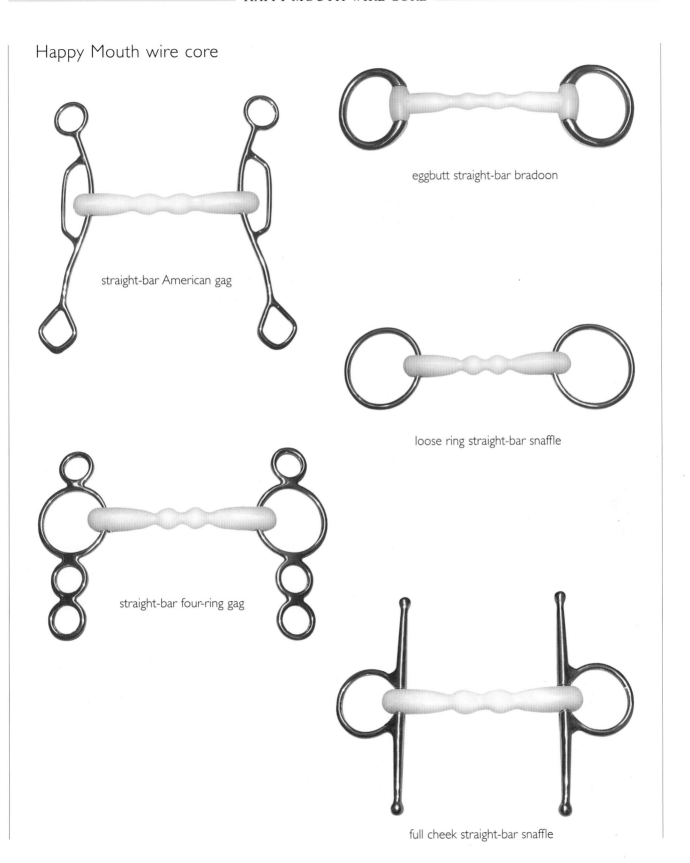

eggbutt straight-bar bradoon

straight-bar American gag

loose ring straight-bar snaffle

straight-bar four-ring gag

full cheek straight-bar snaffle

Happy Mouth steel core

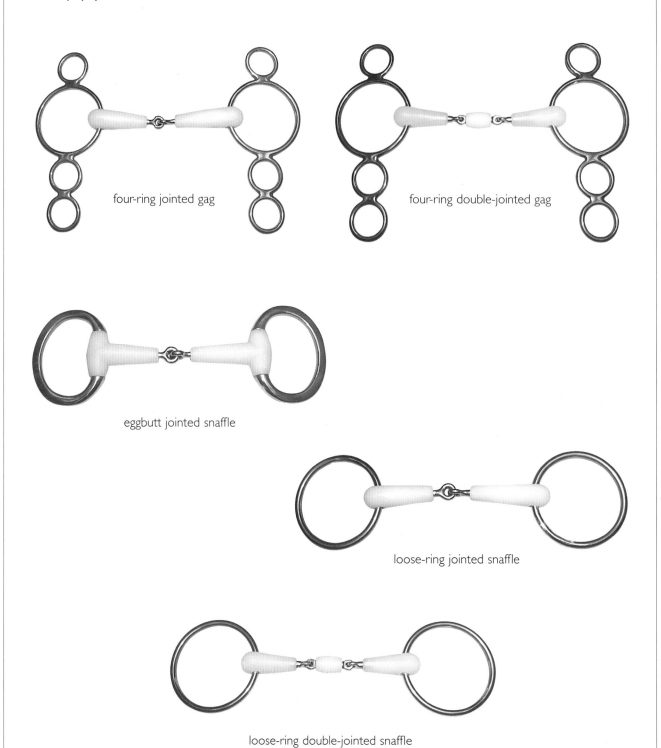

four-ring jointed gag

four-ring double-jointed gag

eggbutt jointed snaffle

loose-ring jointed snaffle

loose-ring double-jointed snaffle

Happy Mouth steel core

full cheek jointed snaffle

full cheek double-jointed
snaffle

Sprenger duo bits

loose-ring snaffle

'Vienna' three-ring

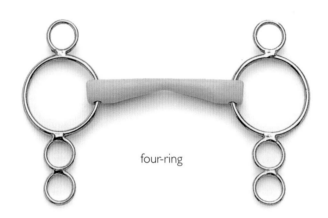

four-ring

butterfly

pelham

Combination hackamore bridles

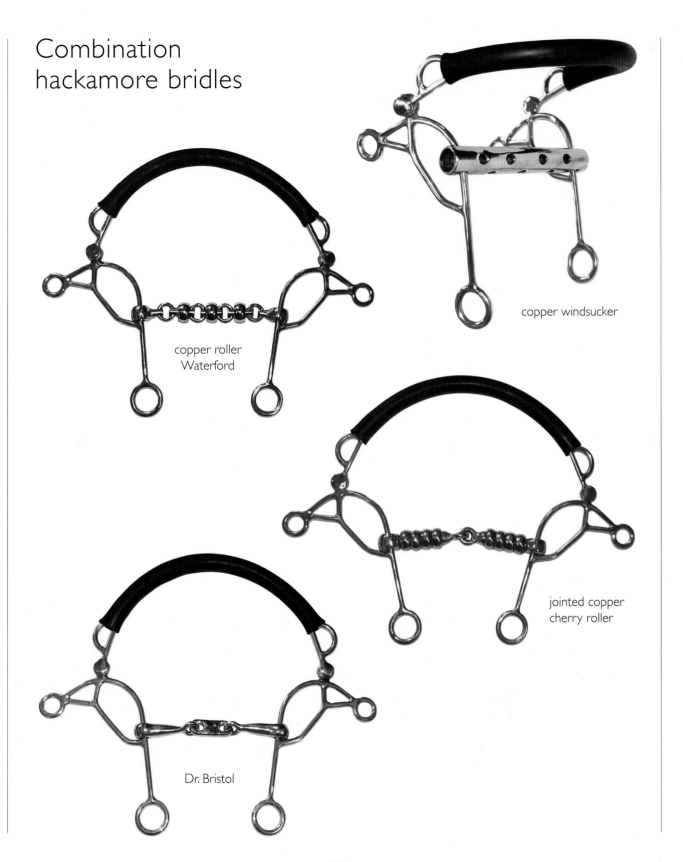

copper windsucker

copper roller
Waterford

jointed copper
cherry roller

Dr. Bristol

Combination hackamore bridles .

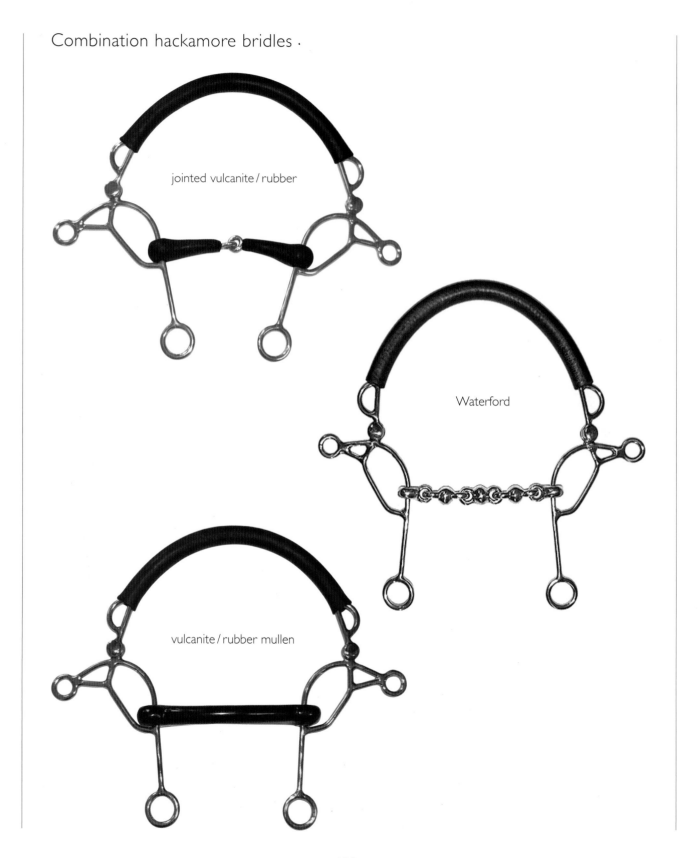

jointed vulcanite / rubber

Waterford

vulcanite / rubber mullen

Elevator

The elevator should be fitted using a bridle with very short cheeks; the bit itself should be fitted comfortably into the corners of the horse's lips in the same way that a snaffle is fitted. It is used mainly with double reins, the top rein having the effect of a snaffle and the bottom rein working on the principle of corner of lip and poll pressure. It is not normally used with a curb chain but some-times with a low-fitting curb strap to prevent the bit from rotating too far. There are two styles of cheek shown. The original pattern cheek is very expensive because of the metal required for the cheeks alone and this style leaves very little room to fit a top rein. The new style comes in a wide variety of mouthpieces.

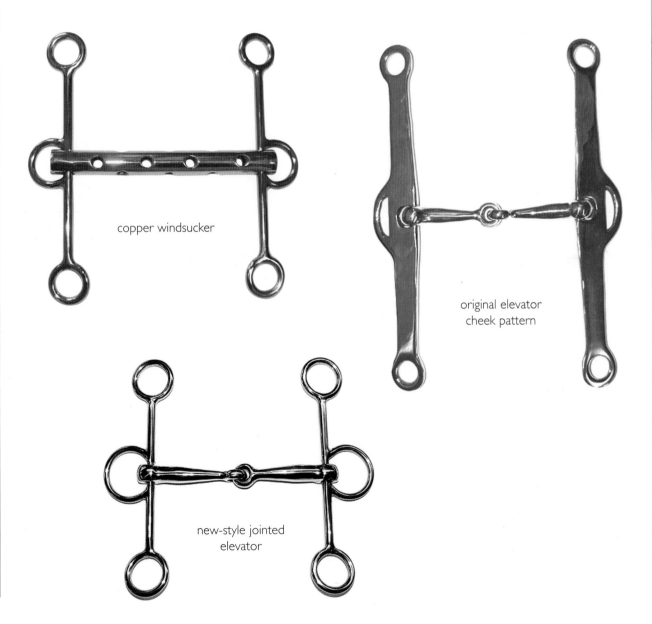

copper windsucker

original elevator
cheek pattern

new-style jointed
elevator

Hackamores

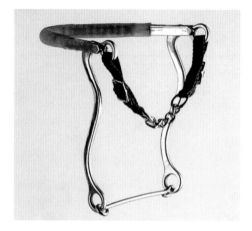

rubber-covered chain nose,
German style

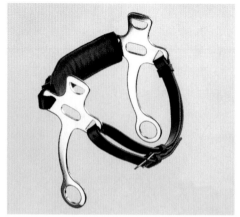

Hackamore, English style

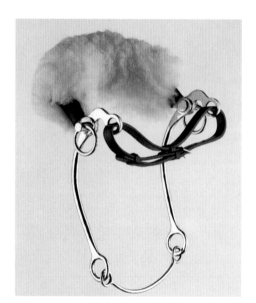

padded lambskin nose, German style

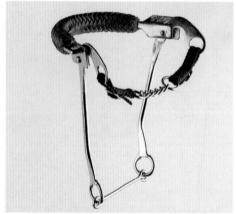

plaited leather nose, German style

Useful Addresses

Distributor of quality English bits

Abbey Saddlery and Crafts,
Marlborough Close,
Parkgate Industrial Estate,
Knutsford,
Cheshire.
Tel: 01565 650343 Fax: 01565 633825

Designer, manufacturer and distributor of Kangaroo bits

John Dewsbury range at:
James Cotterell and Son Ltd.
Bridgeman Street,
Walsall,
West Midlands, WS2 9LS.
Tel: 01922 27331 Fax: 01922 29232

Distributor of Sprenger and KK bits

Buxactic,
The Winnows,
Home Farm,
Sedgwick Park,
Horsham,
West Sussex, RH13 6QE.
Tel: 01403 218880 Fax: 01403 274111

Distributor of Happy Mouth bits

Saddlery Trade Services,
Long Street,
Walsall,
West Midlands, WS2 9DY.
Tel: 01922 630013 Fax: 01922 724355

Supplier of the Scawbrigg bridle

Maurice Savage,
Country Leather Saddlery,
Mount Pleasant Farm,
County Durham,
Tel: 01388 768408

Suppliers of good quality saddlery and bits

Doreen Govan,
Sportack (Montrose),
East Links,
Montrose,
Angus, DD10 8SW.
Tel: 01674 672269

Tally Ho Farm,
Crouch Lane
Winkfield,
Berkshire, SL4 4RZ
Tel: 01344 885373

Index